Fans & Flutterbys

Patricia Knoechel

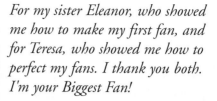

For my sister Eleanor, who showed me how to make my first fan, and for Teresa, who showed me how to perfect my fans. I thank you both. I'm your Biggest Fan!

Cover

A favorite of thrifty quilters since Victorian times, the versatile fan block is especially attractive in small scale florals and oriental fabrics. Springtime flowers from the Rainbow Florals line by Benartex are a pretty choice for this feminine pattern. Another favorite symbol of spring, the butterfly, comes to life as an appliquéd "flutterby," easy to make with fusible interfacing and small scraps. Quilts by Patricia Knoechel, quilting by Teresa Varnes and Carol Selepec.

Inside Front Cover

A lap robe in rose-themed Rainbow Florals fabrics accents this romantic dining room setting. Large scale roses bloom in the fussy cut centers of the fan blocks of the quilt and matching table topper. Quilt by Patricia Knoechel, quilted by Teresa Varnes.

First printing July, 2002

Published by Quilt in a Day®, Inc.
1955 Diamond St, San Marcos, CA 92069

©2002 by Eleanor A. Burns Family Trust

ISBN 1-891776-10-X

Art Director Merritt Voigtlander
Editor Eleanor Burns

Contents

Introduction

What's your fancy? ...Fans or Butterflies

Both are considered traditional symbols of beauty. One is man-made, while the other is one of God's creatures. Both have practical aspects: The fan as a coolant, and the butterfly with its role in the balance of nature. Fans are feminine, while butterflies are whimsical.

The Chinese and Japanese have the longest history of the use of personal fans. The fans produced in the East were true works of art, using painted silk and fine embroidery to depict scenes from nature. Before long, as these decorative fans made their way to Europe, the fan was an absolute necessity for every lady of good taste.

In the Victorian era, the fan was used socially in courtship. Through a gesture with her fan, a young woman could let an admirer know if she was interested or not. The Fan quilt, with its graceful shapes and romantic overtones, was frequently pieced from elegant silks, satins, velvets, ribbons, and lace and was lavishly embellished with beading and embroidery. During the Depression years, the Fan Quilt again gained popularity as a favorite because of its economical use of small and mismatched fabric scraps.

The fan has been called by various names: Victorian Fan, Grandmother's Fan or Oriental Fan. Depending on the use of fabric, color and embellishment, the look is magically transformed to "old fashioned" or elegant! Today, because of the wide array of beautiful floral prints available, the Fan quilt is having a revival yet again.

Another symbol of beauty, the butterfly, is especially at home on a quilt. Harbingers of spring and rebirth, butterflies bring cheer to the heart and eye. Their vivid colors and dancing flight convey a sense of lightness and joy, reminding us not to take things too seriously.

Our pioneers referred to Butterflies as Flutterbys, or Flutterbees, or Sky Kissers. The present name Butterfly, was adapted because of the yellow color in the Sulfer Butterfly. I have always called them Flutterbys, as they often "flutter by" me on my nature walks. With their light graceful wings, they almost appear as tiny angels among us.

Have you decided yet? ...Fans or Butterflies

The Fan Block goes together as quickly as you can wave a fan. The Butterfly Block is more time consuming, yet relaxing. It's a perfect project to take along on your travels.

Have fun as you "flutter about" collecting fabric for your quilt. Creating a quilt is like a "fan" tastic voyage, as you play with shapes, colors and textures. Go into a magical world where anything is possible.

Enjoy the elegant and delightful charm of quilting projects that will bring a little extra color, joy, and harmony into your life.

Patricia Knoechel

Acknowledgements

The special joy of quilting is that it is a shared art. My sister, Eleanor Burns, taught me how to make my first fan twenty years ago. Since then, I have been making fans again and again. Eleanor encouraged me to accentuate my latest fan rendition with the Fan Border and Scallop Border.

My friend, and fellow quilter, Teresa Varnes, shares much of the credit for *Fans & Flutterbys*. With her sewing expertise, we were able to fine-tune the fan techniques.

Although my husband Tom has never made a quilt, he has spent countless hours with me, working on the computer. He took my scribbled words and transformed them into beautiful text.

My special thanks to all of you for your support and inspiration in the process of putting this book together.

Teresa Varnes, Eleanor Burns and Patricia Knoechel

About the Quilts

There are two different patterns in this book, the Fan and the Butterfly.

Fan and Butterfly Settings and Border treatments are interchangeable. Yardage charts begin on page 10.

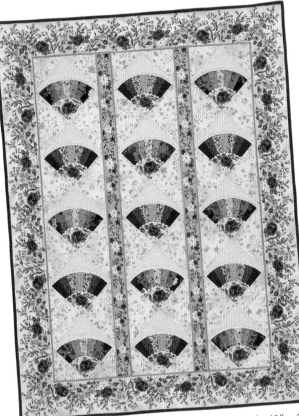

Background Squares
are cut 7" square. Either a Fan or Butterfly is appliqued onto the square.

Side and Corner Triangles
are made from squares cut diagonally. You may use the same fabric as the Background squares, or select a different fabric. These quilts are examples of different Background Squares and Triangles.

Crib Quilt with Stripe Border   *Approximately 42" x 56"*

Lattice
are the strips separating the rows of Fans or Butterflies. Stripe fabric that runs the length of the yardage may be selected, or overall print yardage may also be selected.

"Inside" Lattice
strips separate the vertical rows.

"Outside" Lattice
are the four strips that frame the blocks. Wallhangings, Crib and Lap sizes do not have "outside" Lattice.

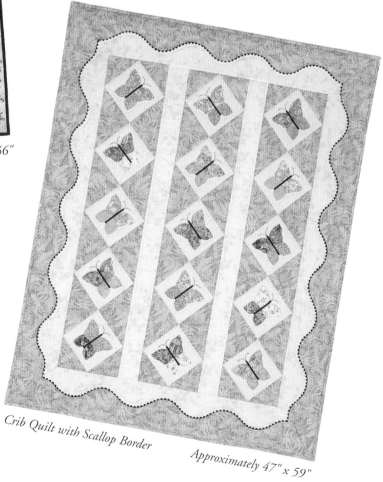

Crib Quilt with Scallop Border

Approximately 47" x 59"

Selecting a Border

Choose any Border for either the Fan or Butterfly. Variations of Borders are given for various sizes of quilts.

Regardless of which Border you select, be certain to check the approximate finished size of quilt against your desired size. There are extreme variations among mattress heights and box springs. The amount of quilting also changes the approximate finished size.

This easy Scrappy Strip Border is for sizes Wallhanging, Crib, and Lap. Yardages are on pages 22-23.

This Fan Border is for experienced quiltmakers in sizes Twin, Double/Queen and King. Yardages are on pages 24-25.

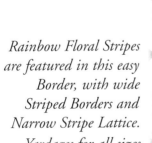

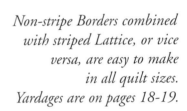

Non-stripe Borders combined with striped Lattice, or vice versa, are easy to make in all quilt sizes. Yardages are on pages 18-19.

Rainbow Floral Stripes are featured in this easy Border, with wide Striped Borders and Narrow Stripe Lattice. Yardages for all sizes are on pages 16-17.

This easy to moderate Scallop Border is for all sizes. Yardages are on pages 20-21.

Selecting Fabric for a Fan Quilt

Select a multi-colored fabric for the Quarter Circles and Borders. From this fabric, select two main Color Families for Fans.

For this example, purple and blue were selected. Half of the Fans will be from the purple Color Family 1 and the other half from the blue Color Family 2. From each Color Family, select four fabrics graduating from dark to light.

Each Fan has a total of seven wedges, with each fabric used two times, except for the center, which is used only one time.

A letter is assigned to each fabric with A being the darkest. The remaining fabrics B, C, and D graduate softly to the center of the Fan, with fabric D being the lightest of the prints.

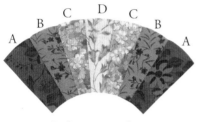

Color Family 1

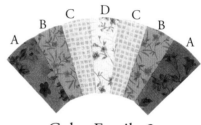

Color Family 2

Variation and Embellishment for Fans

Scrappy Fan

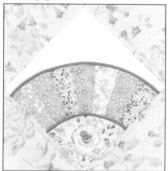

If you prefer a scrappy look, cut (7) 4½" x 8" pieces from a variety of colors and values for every four fans. Trace and layer cut seven wedges from each stack and mix them up.

Rick Rack

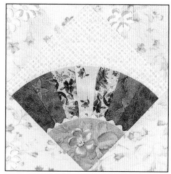

Medium rick rack is available in a variety of colors. Each quilt size lists the required number of 2½ yd packages manufactured by Wrights. This example is white rick rack which has been tea-dyed.

Piping

Piping is available in a variety of colors, and can be purchased in any major fabric store. Each quilt size lists the required number of 2½ yd packages manufactured by Wrights.

Pre-gathered Lace

Pre-gathered Lace should be no wider than ½". Purchase ½ yd lace for each Fan.

Selecting Fabric for a Butterfly Quilt

The Butterfly Quilt was designed to use scraps cut into 6½" squares. Go through your stash and coordinate fabrics in pairs.

Look for fabrics that coordinate, yet contrast with one another. For example, choose fabrics with one color in common, yet different in scale. One fabric may be a medium, while the other is dark or light.

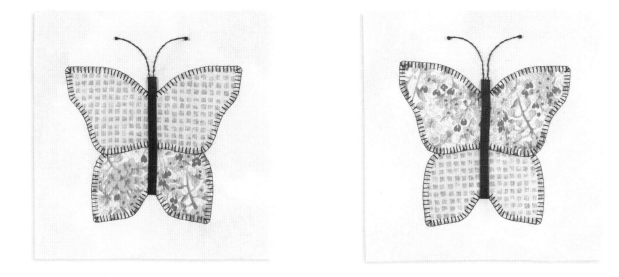

Two different sets of Butterflies are made, with matching tops and bottoms. Then tops are switched to make two different Butterflies.

Refer to your yardage chart and cut one 6½" square for each Butterfly block in your quilt. You can go with bright and bold or pretty pastels. Repeat pairs as desired.

Additional Materials
Light Weight Non-woven Fusible Interfacing is used to finish outside edges of applique. Plain interfacing is widely available, or pre-printed Butterfly fusible can be ordered from Quilt in a Day in panels of six butterflies.

Black Fusible Bias Tape makes a quick Butterfly body, or you may hand or machine embroider a body with black embroidery floss.

Black Embroidery Floss is also used to make feelers.

Wallhanging Fan Blocks or Butterfly Blocks Only — Choose One

Patricia Knoechel

Yardage is based on 40" wide fabric. If your fabric is wider, you may need less fabric. Cut fabric selvage to selvage.

 Background Squares

½ yd
(2) 7" strips cut into
    (6) 7" squares

 Side and Corner Triangles

⅝ yd
(1) 11" strip cut into
    (2) 11" squares
(1) 6" strip cut into
    (4) 6" squares

Or Total

1 yd

Approximate Finished Size 31" x 38"   6 Blocks

Fans ──────────────────────────────

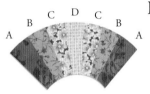 **Fan Color 1 — Three Fans**

A B C
    ⅛ yd each
    (2) 4½" x 7" strips each

D
    ⅛ yd
    (1) 4½" x 7" strip

 Fan Color 2 — Three Fans

A B C
    ⅛ yd each
    (2) 4½" x 7" strips each

D
    ⅛ yd
    (1) 4½" x 7" strip

 Quarter Circles
    ¼ yd
    or (6) "Fussy Cut" Flowers

Rick Rack, Piping or Lace
    (1) 2½ yd pkg or 3 yds

The yardage on this page does not include border fabric.

Butterflies ──────────────────────────────

 Scraps
    (6) 6½" coordinating squares

Fusible Bias Tape
    (1) 11 yd roll
    cut into (6) 6" strips

Fusible Interfacing
    ½ yd
    cut into (6) 6½" squares

Crib Fan Blocks or Butterfly Blocks Only — Choose One

Patricia Knoechel

Yardage is based on 40" wide fabric. If your fabric is wider, you may need less fabric. Cut fabric selvage to selvage.

Background **Squares**	⅔ yd (3) 7" strips cut into (15) 7" squares	
Side and **Corner Triangles**	1 yd (2) 11" strips cut into (6) 11" squares (1) 6" strip cut into (6) 6" squares	
Or Total	1½ yds	

Approximate Finished Size 47" x 59" 15 Blocks

Fans —————————————————————————

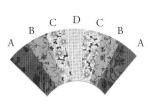

Fan Color 1 — Eight Fans

A B C	⅛ yd each (2) 4½" x 16" strips each
D	⅛ yd (1) 4½" x 16" strip

Fan Color 2 — Seven Fans

A B C	⅛ yd each (2) 4½" x 16" strips each
D	⅛ yd (1) 4½" x 16" strip

Quarter Circles ⅓ yd
or (15) "Fussy Cut" Flowers

Rick Rack, **Piping or Lace** (3) 2½ yd pkgs or 7½ yds

The yardage on this page does not include border fabric.

Butterflies —————————————————————————

Scraps	(16) 6½"coordinating squares
Fusible **Bias Tape**	(1) 11 yd roll cut into (15) 6" strips
Fusible **Interfacing**	1⅛ yds cut into (15) 6½" squares

Lap — Fan Blocks or Butterfly Blocks Only — Choose One

Yardage is based on 40" wide fabric. If your fabric is wider, you may need less fabric. Cut fabric selvage to selvage.

 Background Squares — 1 yd
(4) 7" strips cut into
(18) 7" squares

 **Side and Corner Triangles** — 1¼ yds
(3) 11" strips cut into
(8) 11" squares
(1) 6" strip cut into
(6) 6" squares

Or Total — 2 yds

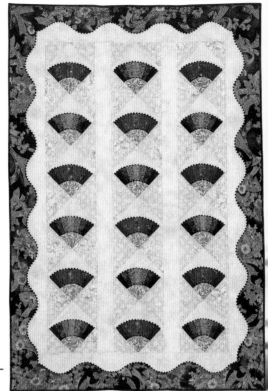

Approximate Finished Size 44" x 63"   18 Blocks

Fans

Fan Color 1 — Nine Fans

A B C — ⅛ yd each
(2) 4½" x 16" strips each

D — ⅛ yd
(1) 4½" x 16" strip

Fan Color 2 — Nine Fans

A B C — ⅛ yd each
(2) 4½" x 16" strips each

D — ⅛ yd
(1) 4½" x 16" strip

Quarter Circles — ¼ yd
or (18) "Fussy Cut" Flowers

Rick Rack, Piping or Lace — (4) 2½ yd pkgs or 9 yds

The yardage on this page does not include border fabric.

Butterflies

 Scraps — (18) 6½" coordinating squares

Fusible Bias Tape — (1) 11 yd roll
cut into (18) 6" strips

Fusible Interfacing — 1¼ yds
cut into (18) 6½" squares

Twin Fan Blocks or Butterfly Blocks Only — Choose One

Yardage is based on 40" wide fabric. If your fabric is wider, you may need less fabric. Cut fabric selvage to selvage.

Background Squares
1⅛ yds
(5) 7" strips cut into
(24) 7" squares

Side and Corner Triangles
1½ yds
(4) 11" strips cut into
(11) 11" squares
(1) 6" strip cut into
(6) 6" squares

Or Total
2⅝ yds

Approximate Finished Size 67" x 99"   24 Blocks

Fans ——————————————————

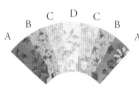

Fan Color 1 — Twelve Fans
A B C
⅛ yd each
(2) 4½" x 20" strips each

D
⅛ yd
(1) 4½" x 20" strip

Fan Color 2 — Twelve Fans
A B C
⅛ yd each
(2) 4½" x 20" strips each

D
⅛ yd
(1) 4½" x 20" strip

Quarter Circles
½ yd
or (24) "Fussy Cut" Flowers

Rick Rack, Piping or Lace
(5) 2½ yd pkgs or 12 yds

The yardage on this page does not include border fabric.

Butterflies ——————————————————

Scraps
(24) 6½" coordinating squares

Fusible Bias Tape
(1) 11 yd roll
cut into (24) 6" strips

Fusible Interfacing
1½ yds
cut into (24) 6½" squares

13

Double/Queen   Fan Blocks or Butterfly Blocks Only — Choose One

Aiko Rogers

Yardage is based on 40" wide fabric. If your fabric is wider, you may need less fabric. Cut fabric selvage to selvage.

 Background Squares   1⅔ yds
(8) 7" strips cut into
   (40) 7" squares

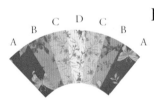 **Side and Corner Triangles**   2⅓ yds
(6) 11" strips cut into
   (18) 11" squares
(2) 6" strips cut into
   (10) 6" squares

Or Total   3⅞ yds

Approximate Finished Size 93" x 112"   40 Blocks

Fans

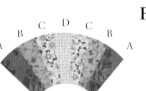 **Fan Color 1 — Twenty Fans**
A B C   ¼ yd each
   (2) 4½" strips each
D   ⅛ yd
   (1) 4½" strip

 Fan Color 2 — Twenty Fans
A B C   ¼ yd each
   (2) 4½" strips each
D   ⅛ yd
   (1) 4½" strip

Quarter Circles   ⅔ yd
or (40) "Fussy Cut" Flowers

Rick Rack, Piping or Lace   (8) 2½ yd pkgs or 20 yds

The yardage on this page does not include border fabric.

Butterflies

 Scraps   (40) 6½" coordinating squares

Fusible Bias Tape   (1) 11 yd roll
cut into (40) 6" strips

Fusible Interfacing   2⅝ yds
cut into (40) 6½" squares

King   Fan Blocks or Butterfly Blocks Only — Choose One

Merritt Voigtlander

Yardage is based on 40" wide fabric. If your fabric is wider, you may need less fabric. Cut fabric selvage to selvage.

Background Squares   2¼ yds
(10) 7" strips cut into
(48) 7" squares

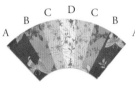

Side and Corner Triangles   2¾ yds
(7) 11" strips cut into
(21) 11" squares
(2) 6" strips cut into
(12) 6" squares

Or Total   4¾ yds

Approximate Finished Size 106" x 114"   *48 Blocks*

Fans

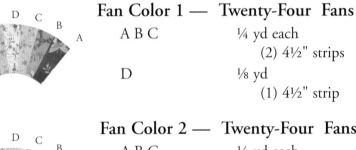

Fan Color 1 — Twenty-Four Fans
A B C   ¼ yd each
(2) 4½" strips
D   ⅛ yd
(1) 4½" strip

Fan Color 2 — Twenty-Four Fans
A B C   ¼ yd each
(2) 4½" strips
D   ⅛ yd
(1) 4½" strip

The yardage on this page does not include border fabric.

Quarter Circles   1 yd
or (48) "Fussy Cut" Flowers

Rick Rack, Piping or Lace   (10) 2½ yd pkgs or 25 yds

Butterflies

Scraps   (48) 6½" coordinating squares

Fusible Bias Tape   (1) 11 yd roll
cut into (48) 6" strips

Fusible Interfacing   3⅛ yds
cut into (48) 6½" squares

Yardage Charts for Borders

Wide and Narrow Stripes

The Rainbow Floral Stripe, designed by Eleanor Burns and manufactured by Benartex, is featured in this book. This stripe is unique, because it can be cut into the Lattice, Outside Borders, and Quarter Circles. For each quilt size, Rainbow Floral Stripe yardage is given.

Alternating stripes run parallel to the selvage and include five 6" wide stripes and four 3" wide stripes. The four narrow stripes make the Lattice. When more than four Lattice are required for a quilt size, the Lattice yardage is doubled. Four of the wide stripes make the four Outside Borders.

The flowers in the extra fifth stripe can be "fussy cut" into quarter circles.

Count out one "fussy cut" flower for each Fan in your quilt. If you can not get your required number of flowers from the extra stripe, you may cut extra flowers from each of the shorter top and bottom border stripes.

Instructions for this border start on page 56.

The Rainbow Floral Border Stripe is used in both the Lattice and Outside Borders. This Border works for all size quilts.

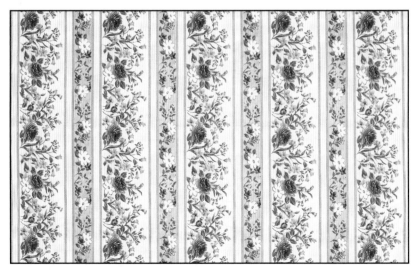

The flowers in the extra fifth stripe can be "fussy cut" into quarter circles.

Alternating stripes run parallel to the selvage and include five 6" wide stripes and four 3" wide stripes.

Wide and Narrow Stripes

Purchase fabric for your Fan or butterfly blocks on pages 10-15.
This chart is for Borders and finishing only.
Except for Border Stripes, cut fabric selvage to selvage.

Approximate Size	Wallhanging 31" x 38"	Crib 42" x 55"	Lap 42" x 64"
Rainbow Floral Stripe 3" Stripe Lattice	1¼ yds 1 repeat	1⅞ yds 2 repeats	2¼ yds 2 repeats
6" Border	4 repeats	4 repeats	4 repeats
Binding	⅜ yd (4) 2¾" strips	½ yd (5) 2¾" strips	⅝ yd (6) 2¾" strips
Backing	1⅛ yds	3 yds	3⅓ yds
Batting	36" x 45"	54" x 66"	55" x 75"

Approximate Size	Twin 61" x 100"	Double/Queen 93" x 110"	King 106" x 114"
Rainbow Floral Stripe 3" Stripe Lattice	3¾ yds 6 repeats	5 yds 8 repeats	6¾ yds 9 repeats
6" Outside Border	4 repeats	4 repeats	4 repeats
Background Border	2 yds (7) 9" strips	3½ yds (9) 13" strips	4⅜ yds (10) 14" strips
Binding	⅞ yd (9) 2¾" strips	1 yd (11) 2¾" strips	1 yd (11) 2¾" strips
Backing	6¼ yds	9 yds	10 yds
Batting	72" x 110"	100" x 118"	115" x 120"

Stripe and Non-stripe

Stripes can be combined with non-stripes for the Lattice and Outside Border. A 3" width is preferred for the Lattice, and a 6" width works well in the Outside Border. Similar widths can be used, but would alter the size and proportion of the quilt slightly.

Overall Non-Stripe fabric can be cut selvage to selvage, and seamed together into lengths. Refer to the Non-stripe column in your yardage chart.

Striped fabric is cut lengthwise with the grain. When purchasing striped yardage, count the number of repeats. If your selected stripe does not have enough repeats across, double the amount of stripe yardage.

Fussy cuts are from any large scale floral print with a 2" to 2½" flower or floral grouping. When purchasing yardage, count out one flower per Fan.

Instructions for this border start on page 56.

This is an example of a Stripe Border and a non-stripe Lattice.   *42" x 64"*

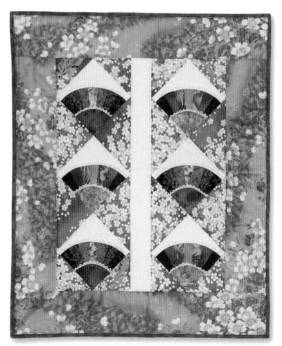

This is an example of a Non-stripe Border and a Non-stripe Lattice.   *32" x 38"*

Stripe and Non-stripe

Purchase fabric for your Fan or Butterfly blocks on pages 10-15.
This chart is for Borders and finishing only.
Except for Border Stripes, cut fabric selvage to selvage.

Approximate Size	Wallhanging 31" x 38"	Crib 44" x 56"	Lap 44" x 67"
Lattice			
3" Stripe	⅞ yd 1 repeat	1⅓ yds 2 repeats	1⅝ yds 2 repeats
or Non-Stripe	⅛ yd (1) 3" strip	⅓ yd (3) 3" strips	⅓ yd (3) 3" strips
Outside Border			
6" Stripe	1¼ yds 4 repeats	1⅞ yds 4 repeats	2¼ yds 4 repeats
or Non-Stripe	¾ yd (4) 6" strips	1 yd (5) 6" strips	1⅛ yds (6) 6" strips
Binding	⅜ yd (4) 2¾" strips	½ yd (5) 2¾" strips	⅝ yd (6) 2¾" strips
Backing	1⅛ yds	3 yds	3⅓ yds
Batting	36" x 45"	54" x 66"	55" x 75"

Approximate Size	Twin 61" x 100"	Double/Queen 93" x 110"	King 106" x 114"
Lattice			
3" Stripe	2¼ yds 6 repeats	2¼ yds 8 repeats	2¼ yds 9 repeats
or Non-Stripe	1 yd (10) 3" strips	1⅜ yds (15) 3" strips	1⅝ yds (18) 3" strips
Background Border	2 yds (7) 9" strips	3½ yds (9) 13" strips	4⅜ yds (10) 14" strips
Outside Border			
6" Stripe	3⅛ yds 4 repeats	3½ yds 4 repeats	3½ yds 4 repeats
or Non-Stripe	1¾ yds (9) 6" strips	2⅛ yds (11) 6" strips	2⅜ yds (12) 6" strips
Binding	⅞ yd (9) 2¾" strips	1 yd (11) 2¾" strips	1 yd (11) 2¾" strips
Backing	6¼ yds	9 yds	9½ yds
Batting	72" x 110"	100" x 118"	115" x 120"

Scallop Border

Crib with Butterflies   *Approximate Finished Size 46" x 58"*

Overall print or plain fabric strips are cut selvage to selvage and then seamed together into lengths for Lattice. Lattice strips are cut 2½" wide to 4½" wide, depending on the quilt size.

The dark Scallop strip is appliqued onto a wider light Border strip. Quilts with a Scallop Border do not have an "Outside" Lattice. This border works for all size quilts.

Instructions for this border begin on page 62.

Scallop Border

Purchase fabric for your Fan or Butterfly blocks on pages 10-15.
This chart is for Borders and finishing only.
Except for Border Stripes, cut fabric selvage to selvage.

Approximate Size	Wallhanging 33" x 40"	Crib 46" x 58"	Lap 46" x 67"
Lattice and Border	1¼ yds	1⅞ yds	1⅞ yds
Lattice	(1) 2½" strip	(3) 3½" strips	(3) 3½" strips
Border	(5) 7" strips	(7) 7" strips	(7) 7" strips
Scallop	1 yd (5) 5½" strips	1¼ yds (7) 5½" strips	1¼ yds (7) 5½" strips
Embellishment	9 yds	10 yds	10 yds
Binding	⅜ yd (4) 2¾" strips	⅝ yd (6) 2¾" strips	⅝ yd (6) 2¾" strips
Backing	1⅛ yds	3 yds	3⅓ yds
Batting	36" x 45"	54" x 66"	55" x 75"

Approximate Size	Twin 70" x 107"	Double/Queen 96" x 107"	King 109" x 107"
Lattice and Border	6½ yds	7½ yds	8¼ yds
Lattice	(4) 4½" strips	(8) 4½" strips	(10) 4½" strips
Border	(11) 18" strips	(12) 18" strips	(13) 18" strips
Scallop	1¾ yds (11) 9" strips	3⅓ yds (12) 9" strips	3⅓ yds (13) 9" strips
Embellishment	12½ yds	15 yds	15 yds
Binding	⅞ yd (9) 2¾" strips	1 yd (11) 2¾" strips	1 yd (11) 2¾" strips
Backing	6¼ yds	9 yds	10 yds
Batting	74" x 114"	100" x 114"	115" x 120"

Scrappy Strip Border

Crib Size Butterfly Quit   *Approximate Finished Size 49" x 61"*

The Quilts have Lattice dividing and framing the rows. A colorful variety of 2½" half-strips are sewn together, and then cut into cross-sections. Because of it's small scale, instructions are given for the Wallhanging, Crib, and Lap sizes only. Choose a stripe fabric with enough repeats for both "Inside" and "Outside" Lattice.

Instructions for this border start on page 70.

Scrappy Strip Border

Purchase fabric for your Fan or Butterfly blocks on pages 10-15.
This chart is for Borders and finishing only.
Except for Border Stripes, cut fabric selvage to selvage.

Approximate Size	Wallhanging 38" x 44"	Crib 49" x 61"	Lap 48" x 70"
Stripe Lattice	1 yd (5) 3" strips	1½ yds (6) 3" strips	1¾ yds (6) 3" strips
or Non-Stripe Lattice	½ yd (5) 3" strips	⅔ yd (7) 3" strips	¾ yd (8) 3" strips
First Border	⅝ yd (4) 4" strips	¾ yd (6) 4" strips	1 yd (6) 4" strips
Scrap Half Strips	(10) 2½" x 22"	(10) 2½" x 44" cut in half	(10) 2½" x 44" cut in half
Binding	½ yd (5) 2¾" strips	⅝ yd (5) 2¾" strips	⅝ yd (6) 2¾" strips
Backing	1⅛ yds	3 yds	3⅓ yds
Batting	42" x 48"	54" x 66"	55" x 75"

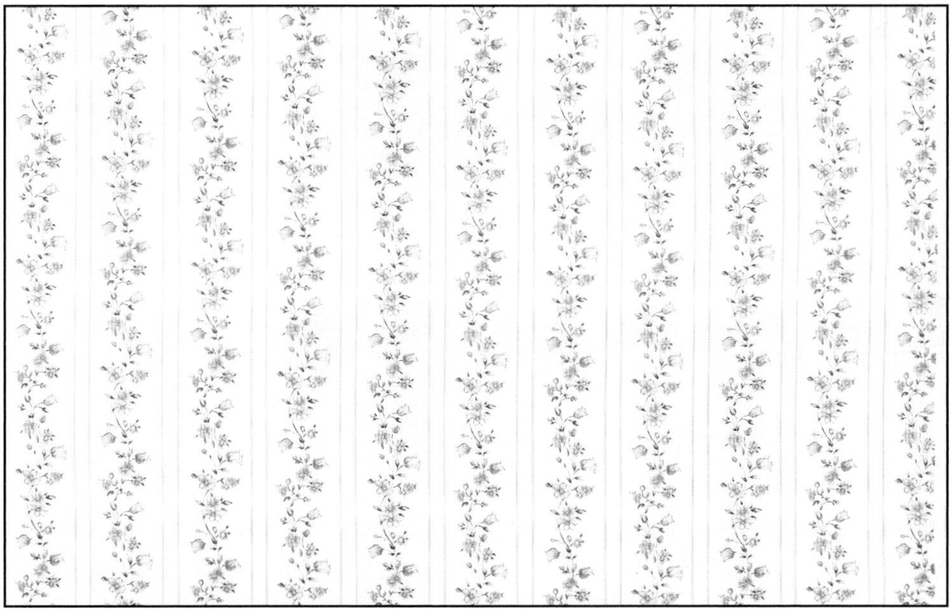

The Anniversary Floral Stripe by Benartex measures 3" across and has twelve repeats. This is a perfect stripe to use for many of your quilts.

Fan Border

Twin Fan Quilt   *Approximate Finished Size 68" x 100"*

Rows of Fans are pieced together with triangles and frame the quilt on three sides only. Smaller Fans are arranged in the four corners. A Table Runner in three different sizes is made using the same technique. This border works for quilt sizes Twin through King.

Instructions for this border begin on page 74.

Fan Border

Purchase fabric for your Fan or Butterfly blocks on pages 10-15.
This chart is for Borders and finishing only.
Except for Border Stripes, cut fabric selvage to selvage.

Approximate Size	Twin 68" x 100"	Double/Queen 90" x 104"	King 104" x 104"
Stripe Lattice*	4½ yds (6) 3" strip	4½ yds (8) 3" strips	6½ yds (9) 3" strips
Background 　Wide Border 　Side Triangles 　Corner Triangles	2¾ yds (8) strips cut later (7) 10" squares (3) 6" squares	4 yds (10) strips cut later (8) 10" squares (3) 6" squares	5 yds (10) strips cut later (9) 10" squares (3) 6" squares
Fan Color 1 　ABC 　D	 ¼ yd each (2) 4½" x 28" strips each ⅛ yd (1) 4½" x 28" strip	 ¼ yd each (2) 4½" strips each ⅛ yd (1) 4½" strip	 ¼ yd each (2) 4½" strips each ⅛ yd (1) 4½" strip
Fan Color 2 　ABC 　D	 ¼ yd each (2) 4½" x 28" strips ⅛ yd (1) 4½" x 28" strip	 ¼ yd each (2) 4½" strips each ⅛ yd (1) 4½" strip	 ¼ yd each (2) 4½" strips each ⅛ yd (1) 4½" strip
Large Quarter Circles or "Fussy Cut" Flowers	⅝ yd (29)	⅔ yd (34)	¾ yd (36)
Small Quarter Circles	⅛ yd	⅛ yd	⅛ yd
Embellishment	6 yds	7 yds	7¼ yds
Facing *(match Backing)*	2 yds (9) 7" strips	2½ yds (11) 7" strips	2¾ yds (12) 7" strips
Backing	6¼ yds	9 yds	10 yds
Batting	72" x 110"	100" x 114"	115" x 120"

*Stripe yardage given is for Rainbow Floral Stripe. If choosing Anniversary Floral Stripe with 12 repeats, only 2¼ yds is needed for any size.

Supplies

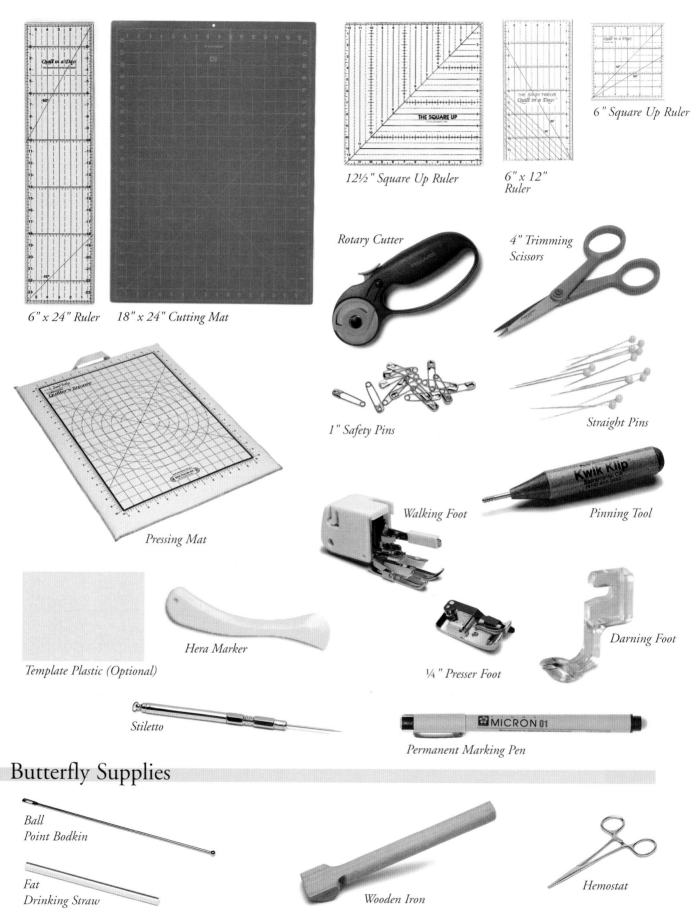

6" x 24" Ruler

18" x 24" Cutting Mat

12½" Square Up Ruler

6" x 12" Ruler

6" Square Up Ruler

Rotary Cutter

4" Trimming Scissors

1" Safety Pins

Straight Pins

Pressing Mat

Walking Foot

Pinning Tool

Template Plastic (Optional)

Hera Marker

¼" Presser Foot

Darning Foot

Stiletto

Permanent Marking Pen

Butterfly Supplies

Ball Point Bodkin

Fat Drinking Straw

Wooden Iron

Hemostat

Cutting

Cutting Non-Stripe Strips

1. Cut a nick in one selvage, the tightly woven edge on both sides of the fabric. Tear across the grain from selvage to selvage. Press.

2. Fold the fabric in half, matching the frayed edges. Don't worry about the selvages not lining up correctly as this is not always possible. Line up the straight of the grain.

3. Place the fabric on the gridded mat with the folded edge along a horizontal line, and the torn edge on a vertical line.

4. Place the quarter inch line of the ruler along the torn edge of the fabric.

5. Spread your fingers and place four on top of the ruler with the little finger on the edge to keep the ruler firmly in place.

6. Take the rotary cutter in your free hand and open the blade. Starting below the fabric, begin cutting away from you, applying pressure on the ruler and the cutter. Keep the blade next to the ruler's edge.

7. Check your yardage chart for widths of strips to cut.

Cutting Striped Fabric

1. Lay out stripe fabric. Place 6" x 24" ruler's ¼" line on edge of stripe for seam allowance. Rotary cut one side of stripe the length of fabric.

2. Place ¼" line on opposite side of stripe, and cut.

Cutting Side and Corner Triangle Squares

1. Fold fabric in fourths, matching the folded edge with the selvage edge.

2. Lay fabric on cutting mat with most of it to the right. Line up the top edge of fabric with horizontal line on mat.

3. Line up the right edge of a 12½" Square Up ruler with vertical line of mat, and trim for a clean straight edge.

4. Reposition ruler, and line up 11" line on cut edge. Cut strip.

5. Open strip once so strip is approximately 21" wide.

6. Square off selvage edges. Layer cut 11" squares.

7. Open remaining part of strip. Cut one 11" square.

8. From the remaining 11" strip, cut one 6" square.

9. Cut 6" strips into your remaining number of 6" squares.

Yardage charts are based on getting three 11" squares for Side Triangles from one 11" strip. From the remaining 11" strip, cut one 6" square. If you have a 45" wide piece of fabric, and can cut four 11" squares from one strip, you can cut less strips.

Fold fabric in fourths, and straighten left edge.

Cut 11" strips.

Open 11" strip, and trim selvage edge. Cut (3) 11" squares and (1) 6" square.

Cutting Non-Fussy Quarter Circles

1. Straighten edge of fabric. Layer cut pieces with fabric folded in half.

2. Punch out pattern from back of book.

3. Trace two quarter circles side by side.

4. Cut the straight edges with a rotary cutter and the curved edges with scissors.

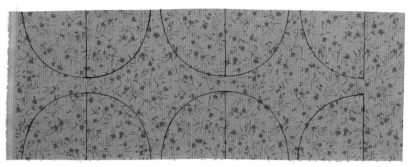

Keep square corners on straight of grain.

Fussy Cutting Quarter Circles

1. Trace a quarter circle on template plastic and cut out. *The pattern is on page 103.*

2. Center the quarter circle template on one flower and trace the outside edge of the flower onto the template.

3. Trace the quarter circle on the fabric.

4. Line up the flower lines with the next flowers, and trace the quarter circles.

5. Cut the straight edges with a rotary cutter, and the curved edges with scissors.

Note the way the alternating flowers turn in opposite directions, and turn the template accordingly.

Keep square corners on straight of grain.

Making Fans

Cutting Fan Wedges

1. Start with 4½" strips of Fan Color 1, and then repeat with Fan Color 2. Refer to your yardage chart for the cutting length of strips A, B, C, and D.

2. Lay out all seven strips in this order: A,B,C,D,C,B,A.

3. **Starting on the left side**, flip B right sides together to A.
Flip D to C.
Flip B to C.

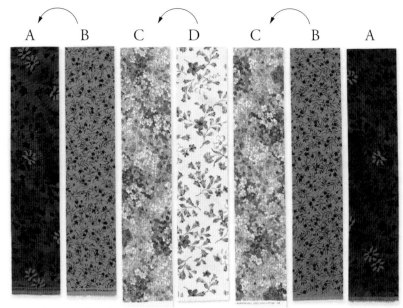

A B C D C B A

For a Scrappy Fan, lay out seven different strips.

Stack all strips in one pile from left to right, keeping A/B on top.

A/B   C/D   C/B   A

4. Working from **left to right,** stack all strips into one pile. **Keep pair A/B on top, and single strip A on the bottom.**

5. Press the stack so the pieces stay together while cutting.

6. Place the stack horizontally on a cutting mat. The pieces are now stacked in their cutting and sewing order.

7. Remove large Wedge template from the back of the book.
   The Small Fan templates are used in the Fan Border and Table Runner.

8. With a permanent marking pen, center and trace the Wedge template onto the top **strip, which should be the wrong side of Fabric B.**
   Alternate direction of template, with Wedges placed side by side and sharing same lines.
   Each stack of Wedges makes one Fan.

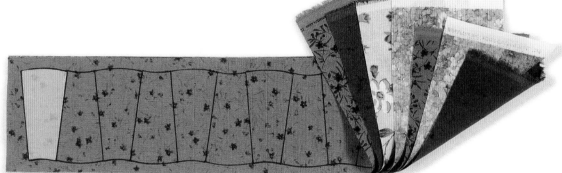

Wrong side of Fabric B is on top. The pieces are now stacked in their cutting and sewing order.

9. Trace this number of Wedges.

	Fan Color 1	Fan Color 2
Wallhanging	3	3
Crib	8	7
Lap	9	9
Twin	12	12
Double/Queen	20	20
King	24	24

10. Layer cut along the straight lines with a rotary cutter and ruler.

Apply heavy pressure with sharp rotary cutter, and cut through seven layers.

11. Cut along the curved edges with sharp scissors. As each stack is cut, place on a ruler in staggered order for transporting to sewing machine.

With sharp scissors, cut along curved edge.

Directional Fabric Option

1. On single 4½" strip of directional fabric, trace and cut wedges equal to half the number of Fans needed.

2. Carefully remove the wedge of directional fabric from stacks cut upside down and replace with wedge cut right side up.

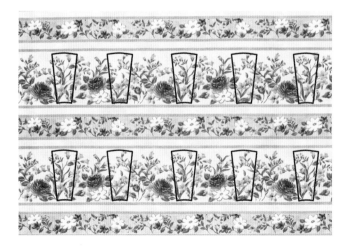

Sewing Fan Wedges

Sew with ¼" seam allowance and 15 stitches per inch.

1. Begin assembly-line sewing by feeding the first pair A/B from the top of the stack. Butt pair C/D and continue stitching. Follow with pair C/B.

2. When you come to single Fabric A, **do not sew it at this time.** Remove it from the stack and begin a new stack with all the A's.

   *Before sewing all pairs from the stack, **make one Fan** to test your seam allowance as explained on page 37. If necessary, correct seam allowance and then assembly-line sew all Fans.*

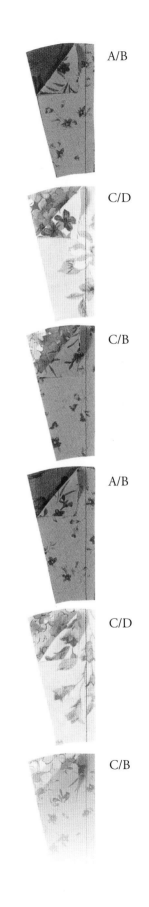

A/B

C/D

C/B

A/B

C/D

C/B

3. Clip pairs apart and stack in order in three separate stacks.

4. Stack A/B pairs and C/D pairs.

5. Flip pair C/D onto an A/B pair and stitch. Continue assembly-line sewing all pairs of C/D to A/B pairs.

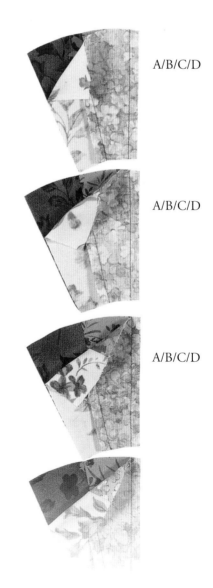

6. Continue with the stack of C/B pairs and the stack of A's.

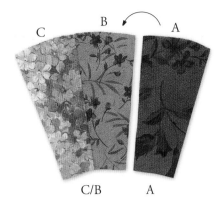

7. Flip an A onto a C/B pair. Stitch, and continue assembly-line sewing all A's to C/B pairs.

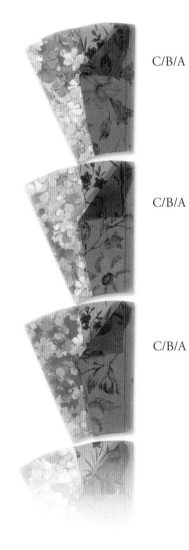

8. Place the stack of A/B/C/D next the stack of C/B/A's. Flip and sew all wedges together.

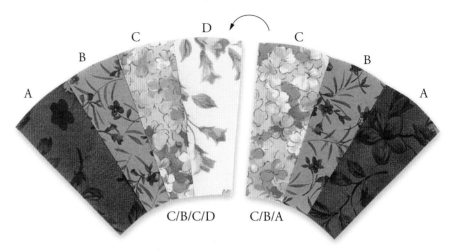

9. From wrong side, gently press all seams to left. Press on right side to eliminate any folds.

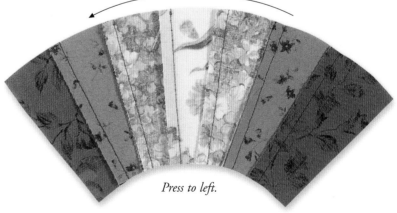

Press to left.

10. Place one Fan on a 7" Background Square to test the accuracy of your seam allowance. When seams are an accurate ¼", edges of Fan line up with Background Square. As much as ⅛" extending over the edge **can be trimmed later.**

If Fan extends over Background square, trim after adding embellishment.

Embellishment Options

Finish outside edges with one of these options.
1. Rick Rack
2. Piping
3. Pre-gathered Lace

Sewing Rick Rack

1. Place a clear multi-purpose or applique foot on sewing machine.

2. Line up the highest peak of the rick rack with the top edge of the Fan. With a **scant ¼" seam allowance** and 2.8 stitches per inch, sew through the center of the rick rack, yet closer to the highest peaks. Use needle down position if available.

3. Assembly-line sew rick rack from one Fan and Quarter Circle to the next.

4. Use one hand to turn under the top peaks of rick rack while pressing with the other hand.

5. Press under top edge of rick rack on Quarter Circles.

Sewing Purchased Piping

1. Place a clear multi-purpose or zipper foot on sewing machine. Some machines will handle the piping better than others. With a multi-purpose foot, the piping will require a little coaxing when starting out.

2. For greater flexibility, trim 1/16" to 1/8" from the raw edge of the piping.

3. Set your stitch length on 12 stitches per inch or 2.5. Line up the raw edge of the piping with the outside edge of the Fan. Stitch on the piping stitches, or along the right edge of the stitches.

4. Assembly-line sew from one Fan and Quarter Circle to the next.

5. Finger press raw edges under.

Hand made piping (Optional)
Make your own piping by cutting contrasting fabric into 1" bias strip, and pressing in half wrong sides together. You need 1/2 yd for every Fan.

Sewing Lace

1. Place a clear multi-purpose foot on sewing machine. Set your stitch length to 12 stitches per inch or 2.5. Use needle down position if available.

2. Place the lace right sides together with top edge of Fan. Line up straight edge of lace with edge of the Fan. Stitch along the left edge of the stitches on lace.

3. Assembly-line sew from one Fan and Quarter Circle to the next.

4. Press, or finger press the binding under. Avoid a hot iron which can melt nylon lace.

Background Squares

1. Place 7" Background Squares on corner of pressing mat. Arrange Wedges with both sides equal distance from corners of Background. Use lines on mat for measurement.

2. With pins standing straight up, pin through the ditch on embellishment.

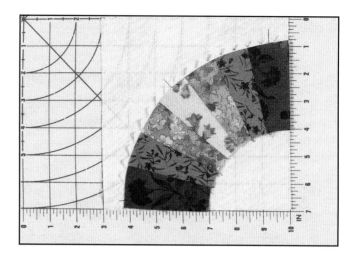

Quarter Circles

1. Position Quarter Circle in lower corner, **overlapping bottom edge of Fan**. Stand pins through embellishment.

2. Gently lift up block and re-insert pins one at a time.

3. With matching or invisible thread, stitch in the ditch on embellishment. Use needle down position and 10 stitches per inch, or 3.0 to prevent puckers. If puckering occurs, you may lessen tension.

4. Stitch top edge of all Fans and Quarter Circles, and press.

5. Turn block to wrong side and sliver trim any excess Fan extending beyond edge of square.

Stitch top edge of all Fans and Quarter Circles.

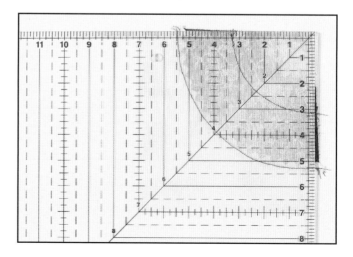

Sewing Blocks Together

Cutting Side and Corner Triangles

1. Cut 11" squares on both diagonals, making four Side Triangles per square.

2. Cut 6" squares on one diagonal, making two Corner Triangles per square.

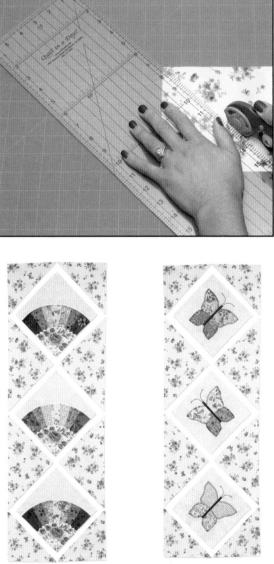

Laying Out Vertical Rows

1. Lay out Fan or Butterfly blocks with Side and Corner Triangles according to your size quilt. (Pages 44-45.)

2. On Fan quilts, alternate between Fan Color 1 and Fan Color 2. On each successive vertical row, alternate the color of the Fan.

3. On Butterfly quilts, alternate between Butterflies turning to right, and turning to left.

Quilt Layouts

Wallhanging 2 x 3

Crib 3 x 5

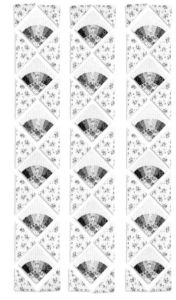

Lap 3 x 6

Twin 3 x 8

(12) 6" squares
(9) 11" squares

Day Bed Twin 4 x 6

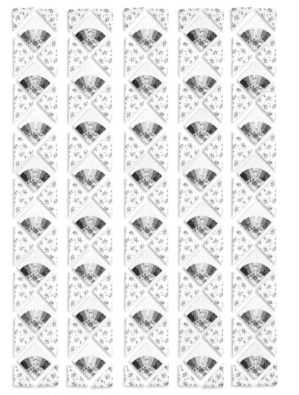

Double/Queen 5 x 8

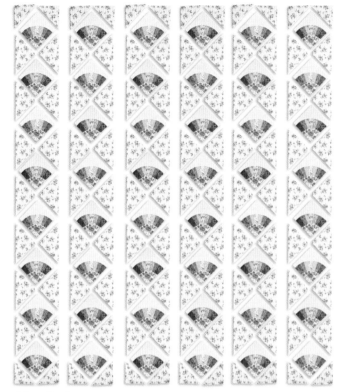

King 6 x 8

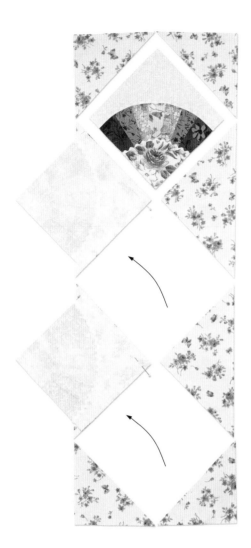

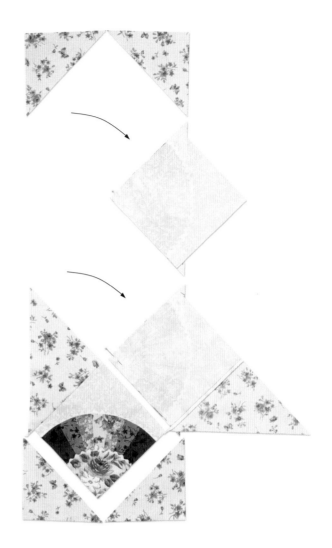

4. Starting with the second block from the top, flip blocks up to the left. Match up square corners and pin with tip extending at bottom. Stack paired blocks and assembly-line sew with bias edge on bottom to prevent stretching.

5. Clip blocks apart and press with triangles on top. Return to layout.

6. Starting at the top, flip blocks down to the right. Leave last block in layout. Match up square corners and pin. Stack paired blocks and assembly-line sew, starting from the square corners.

7. Clip blocks apart and press with triangles on top.

 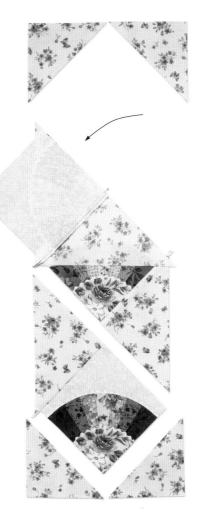 

8. Return to layout.

9. Flip top row down to second row. Match center seam, pin, and sew. Continue adding remaining rows in this manner.

10. Press diagonal seams down towards bottom of quilt.

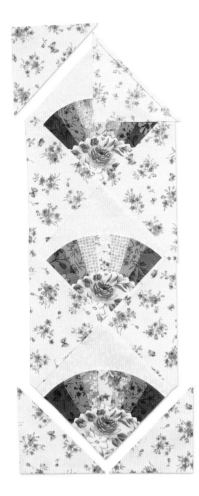

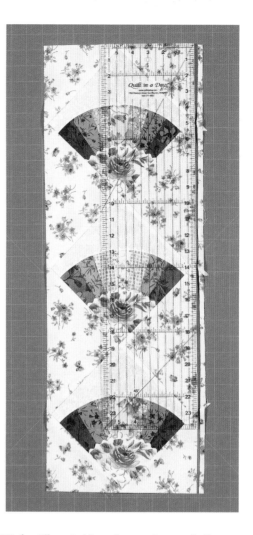

11. With tips extending, flip Corner Triangles onto block. Pin in place, and sew with triangle on bottom. Press with triangle on top. Add remaining corners in same manner.

12. With 6" x 24" ruler, trim ¼" from points where seams cross.

13. Sew remaining vertical rows. Alternate first block in each row.

Adding Lattice Strips

Choose between a Stripe Lattice or Non-stripe Lattice.

Cutting Striped Lattice

1. Measure length of vertical rows. Cut Lattice strips 1" longer than vertical rows.

2. Lay out stripe fabric. Place 6" x 24" ruler's ¼" line on edge of stripe for seam allowance. Rotary cut one side of stripe the length of fabric.

3. Place ¼" line on opposite side of stripe, and cut.

Piecing Non-stripe Lattice

1. Square selvage edges.

2. Sew together into one long strip.

3. Cut Lattice strips 1" longer than vertical rows.

Laying Out Vertical Rows with Lattice

1. Lay out vertical rows with Lattice according to your size quilt and selected Border. Alternate the first block in each row.

   Inside Lattice strips separate the vertical rows.
   Outside Lattice are the four strips that frame the blocks.

Wallhanging, Crib, Lap

Smaller quilts with a Stripe Border or Scallop Border have Inside Lattice only.

Quilts finished with a Scrappy Strip Border have both Inside and Outside Lattice.

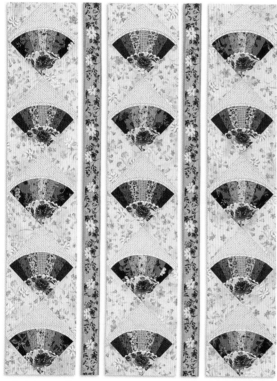

Crib Example

Crib Example

Twin, Double/Queen, King Size

Larger quilts with Stripe Border or Fan Border have both Inside and Outside Lattice.

Larger quilts with a Scallop Border have Inside Lattice only.

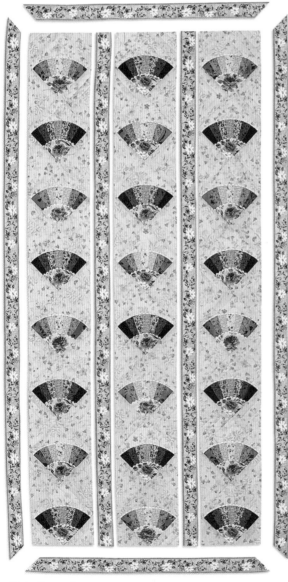

Twin Example

Twin Example

2. Place Inside Lattice strips between the rows. Place carefully if Lattice strips are directional or pattern needs centering. Position strip to extend about ½" at each end.

3. Starting with Lattice to right of Row One, flip Lattice onto row.

Wallhanging example

4. Sew Lattice to blocks with accurate ¼" seam. If using striped Lattice, sew along stripe line.

5. Press with Lattice on top.

6. **Crib and Larger Size Quilts:** Continue adding Lattice to the right side of rows.

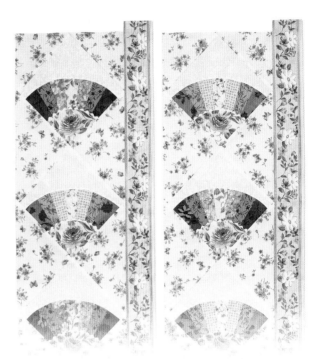

7. Place vertical rows upside down, with Lattice on left of blocks.

8. Line up edges of Fans.

9. Flip Row Two to left onto Row One.

10. Line up top and bottom edges of rows to check for consistency in length. Pin edge of Lattice to edge of Fan so Fans line up.

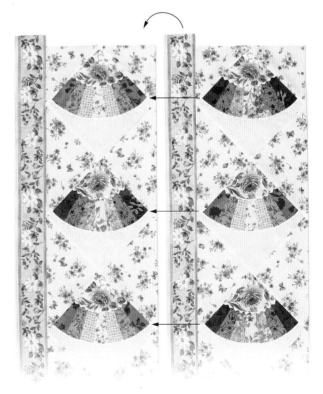

11. Pin Lattice in place at top and bottom. If necessary, ease to fit. Sew Lattice with an accurate ¼" seam, or along stripe line.

12. Sew all rows together. Trim excess Lattice from ends.

13. Place quilt on your bed. Estimate the finished size with planned Borders. You may desire to change or add more Borders.

14. Finish according to your selected Border.

Stripe or Non-Stripe Border
Wallhanging, Crib, or Lap
    Turn to page 56.
Twin and Larger Quilts
    Sew Outside Lattice to quilt.
    Continue with First Border.

Scallop Border
Wallhanging, Crib, or Lap
    Turn to page 62.

Twin and Larger Quilts
    Turn to page 62.

Scrappy Strip Border
Wallhanging, Crib, or Lap
    Sew Outside Lattice to quilt. Continue with First Border.
    Turn to page 70.

Fan Border
Twin and Larger Quilts
    Sew Outside Lattice.
    Turn to page 74.

Adding First Border

1. Cut Border strips to desired width. Refer to Yardage Charts, pages 16-25.

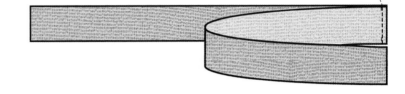

2. Trim away the selvages at a right angle.

3. Lay the first strip right side up. Lay the second strip right sides to it. Backstitch, stitch, and backstitch again.

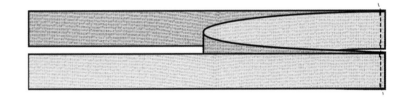

4. Continue assembly-line sewing all the short ends together into long pieces.

5. Cut Border pieces the average length of both sides.

6. Pin and sew to the sides. Fold out and press seams toward Border.

7. Measure the width and cut Border pieces for the top and bottom. Pin and sew. Press seams toward the Border.

8. Turn to your Selected Border.

Stripe or Non-stripe Border page 56.
Scallop Border page 62.
Scrappy Strip Border page 70.
Fan Border page 74.

Stripe and Non-Stripe Borders with Mitered Corners

Rainbow Floral Stripes Only

Wallhanging, Crib, and Lap Size: Position Rainbow Floral Stripe with Large Flowers toward inside edge. See example on this page.

Twin Size and Larger Quilts: Position Rainbow Floral Stripe with Large Flowers toward outside edge. As quilt hangs on bed, flowers appear to be growing up from the floor. See example on page 56.

Non-Stripe Borders are sewn to quilt top in same manner as striped border, and corners are mitered.

1. Calculate the length of the strip. The total length includes length of the quilt, plus two times the width of the strip, plus 6" inches at each end to match the flower or design in the corner.

2. Cut the strip. Before cutting off end of the strip, lay out the long side strips next to the quilt.

3. At a 45° angle, turn under one end of the strip to see where the seam will fall. Ideally the seam will not fall on a large flower.

4. Lay out top and bottom strip. Fold back corners to check placement. Adjust if necessary, and cut length of strips.

Position stripe with a flower at each end.

5. Flip a side strip onto the quilt. On the wrong side of the strip, mark a dot ¼" in from the top and bottom edges of the quilt. Continue making dots on remaining side border.

6. Lockstitch on dot, and sew along the line printed on the fabric.

7. Stop sewing on the dot ¼" up from the bottom edge of the quilt, and lockstitch.

Mark dot ¼" down from top edge of quilt.

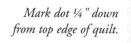

8. In same manner, sew strip to opposite side of quilt.

9. Sew top and bottom strips to quilt. Start and stop on dots.
   Seams will meet side strips ¼" in from edges.

Mitered Corner

1. Fold quilt up diagonally to line up two strips right sides together.

2. Line up the diagonal line on a 12½" Square Up ruler with the outside edge of the strips. Line up the right edge of the ruler with the dot where the stitches meet.

3. Draw a sewing line from the outside edge to the dot.

Line up the right edge of the ruler with the dot where the stitches meet.

4. Place pins at the points where the drawn line crosses the fabric line. Check pin alignment with the second strip underneath.

5. Starting at the outside edge, stitch along the drawn line to the dot, and lockstitch.

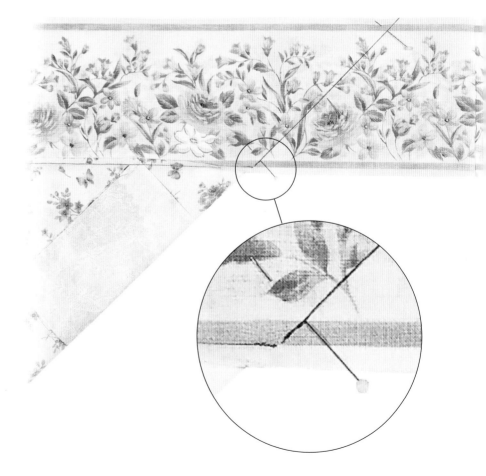

6. Trim seam allowance to ½" and press seams open.

7. Miter all four corners in this manner.

8. Press seams toward Border.

Scallop Border with Non-stripe Lattice

Scallop Border with Non-stripe Lattice

Non-stripe Lattice Strips must be cut exactly to size given on your yardage chart in order for Scallops to meet in the corners.

Wallhanging, Crib, and Lap Quilts

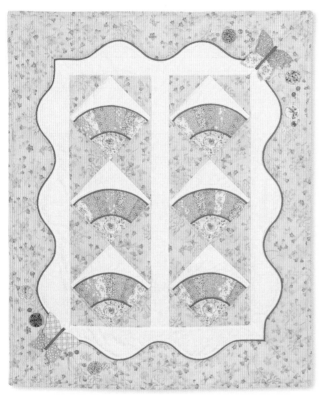

Wallhanging Example   *Patricia Knoechel*

Twin, Double/Queen, and King Quilts

Twin Example   *Teresa Varnes*

1. Sew 5½" Scallop strips together into one long continuous strip. Press seams open.

2. Sew 7" Border strips together into one long continuous strip. Press seams open.

1. Sew 9" Scallop strips together into one long continuous strip. Press seams open.

2. Sew 18" Border strips together into one long continuous strip. Press seams open.

3. Punch out the Scallop template in back of book. Add 3½" height to template for Twin, Double/Queen, and King.

4. Begin on the left end of the Scallop strip and allow for the Mitered Corner. If you are left handed, start on the right.

Wallhanging, Crib and Lap:
Measure 10" in from the end and place a dot along the top edge.

Twin, Double/Queen, and King:
Measure 21" in from the end and place a dot along the top edge.

5. Line up the left edge of the template with the dot. Line up the bottom edge of the template with the bottom of the fabric.

6. With a pencil or fine permanent pen, trace along the top curved edge of the template. Mark dot on the right top edge of the template.

7. Pick up template and shift to the right of the dot. Trace the curved top edge. Continue tracing the template according to the total number of Valleys listed for your size quilt.

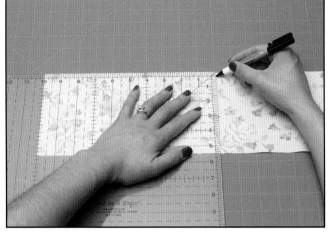

Measure in 10" from end for Wallhanging, Crib, and Lap, and 21" from end on Twin, Double/Queen, and King quilts.

Scallop template is 5¼" deep for Wallhanging, Crib and Lap quilts, and 8¾" deep for Twin, Double/Queen, and King quilts.

When the template is traced side by side, a scallop is created.

8. **Allow an additional 10" or 21" at the opposite end for the Mitered Corner. Cut off end.**

9. Trace two identical side strips, and identical top and bottom strips.

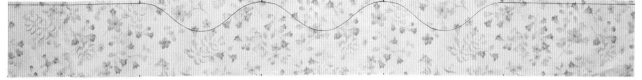

This is an example of three valleys for Wallhanging Sides. Allow 10" on each end for miter.

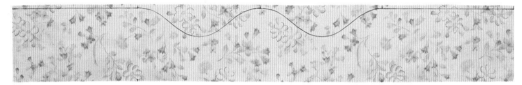

This is an example of two valleys for Wallhanging Top and Bottom.

	Two Side Strips	Top and Bottom
Wallhanging	3 Valleys	2 Valleys
Crib	5 Valleys	4 Valleys
Lap	6 Valleys	4 Valleys
Twin	9 Valleys	5 Valleys
Double/Queen	9 Valleys	8 Valleys
King	9 Valleys	9 Valleys

10. Cut along traced Scallop lines. Trim ¼" off the top edge of the 10" or 21" miter allowance at each end.

11. With scant ¼" seam allowance, sew embellishment along the top edge of the strip. Turn the top edge under and press.

12. If using piping, clip two V's on the inside curves.

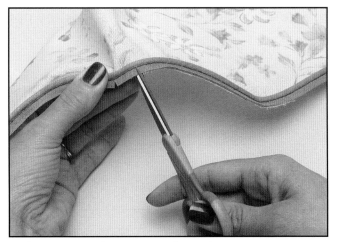

If using piping, clip two V's on the inside curves.

13. Cut four Background strips to the same length as the four Scallop strips. Place Scallop strips on top of Background strips, lining up straight edges along the bottom.

14. Place paired strips on pressing mat. **Measure the distance from top edge of Background strip to top edge of Scallop fabric. For a perfect miter, this distance should measure exactly the same on all Border strips. Adjust placement as necessary.**

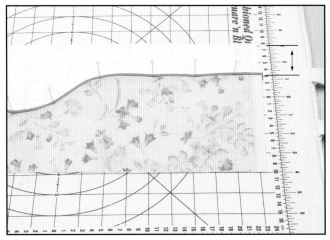

This distance should measure exactly the same on all Border strips.

15. Place pins **standing straight up in ditch** at embellishment.

16. Working from one end, carefully pick up strip and re-insert pins, one at a time. Pin bottom edge of strips.

17. With matching thread, needle down position, and 3.0 stitches per inch, stitch in the ditch along embellishment.

18. To secure the bottom, top stitch less than ¼" in from edges.

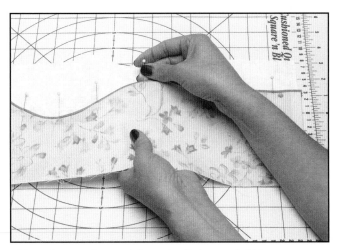

Place pins standing straight up in ditch at embellishment.

Side Borders

1. Mark a dot ¼" in on all four corners of quilt.

2. Fold the side strips in half lengthwise wrong sides together. Place a pin at the center. Match the center Valley with the center of quilt.

3. From the center out, pin the Borders in place with strips extending at ends to allow for mitered corners.

4. Sew a ¼" seam, beginning and ending stitches ¼" in from the ends of the quilt.

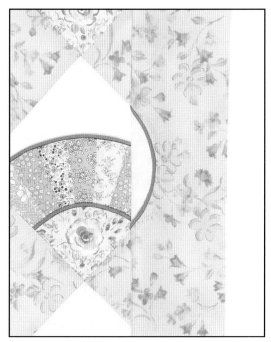

Fold back strip and center Valley with block.

Top and Bottom Borders

1. Center and pin strips in place.

2. Begin and end sewing ¼" in from ends.

Mitered Corners

1. Fold quilt up diagonally, and line up two adjacent Border strips right sides together.

2. Line up 45° diagonal line on 12½" Square Up ruler, or 6" x 24" ruler with outside edges of the strips.

   Line up the point where the stitches meet with the bottom right edge of the ruler.

3. Draw a sewing line from the outside edge to the point where the stitches meet. Place several pins on the drawn line.

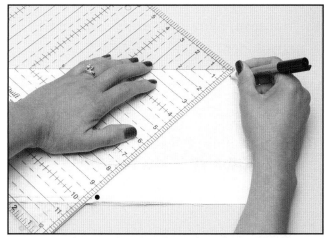

Line up 45° line on edge of Border to draw diagonal line for miter.

4. "Stand" a pin at the point where the drawn line crosses the stitching line. Align with the stitches of the strip underneath.

5. To prevent shifting, insert a second pin just beside the "standing pin". Remove the "standing pin."

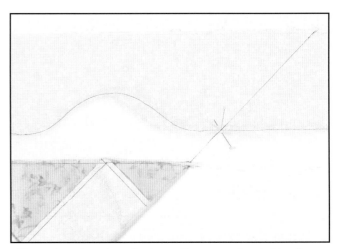

Pin at the point where the drawn line crosses the stitching line.

6. **Piping:** To eliminate the bulk of double piping, clip piping about ½" outside the miter line. With hemostats or tweezers, pull about 1" cording from piping and trim. Repeat on opposite piping.

7. Starting at the outside edge, stitch along the drawn line, stop ¼" from the end, and lockstitch.

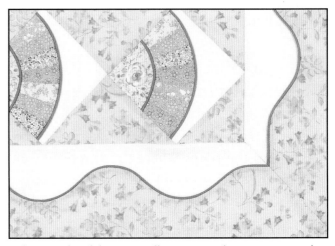

To eliminate bulk, clip piping on part of miter that will be trimmed away after sewing. Pull 1" cording from piping and trim.

8. Trim seam allowance to ½", and press seams open.

9. Miter all four corners in this manner.

10. Turn to Finishing your Quilt on page 104.

The two sides of the miter will not necessarily mirror one another.

Dimensional Butterfly

1. Reduce Butterfly templates on copy machine to 85%.

2. Follow Butterfly sewing and turning on pages 96-100. Use a second piece of fabric for backing instead of interfacing.

3. Cut a 5" length of untrimmed piping and remove cording.

4. Pin Butterfly on Mitered Corner. Line up center of piping with center of Butterfly.

5. Stitch down center of piping, leaving the ends unstitched to tuck under at top and bottom. Turn folded edge over raw edge like bias binding. Hand stitch folded edge and tuck ends under.

6. Optional embellishments include yo-yo's and buttons.

Scrappy Strip Border

1. Lay out the ten half-strips in a pleasing order, with selvages at bottom.

   Crib and Lap Size: Repeat with second set of half-strips.

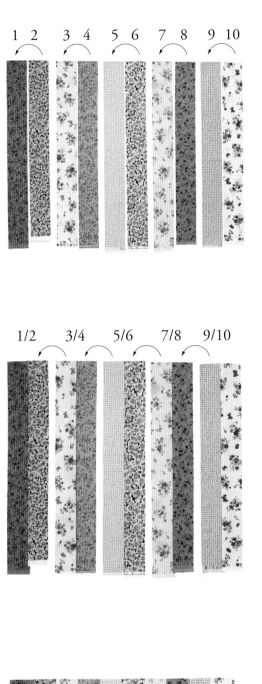

2. Assembly-line sew strips together in pairs. Set seams with **even number strips on top.** Open, and press.

3. Sew pairs together and press all seams in same direction. Press out folds at the seam lines.

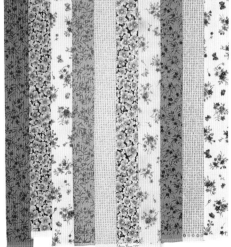

4. Cut 2½" sections for your size quilt.

	Sections
Wallhanging	8
Crib	12
Lap	14

Cut into 2½" sections.

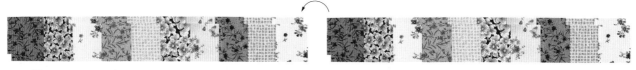

Wallhanging Example: Sew two sections together for each side.

5. Sew 2½" sections together, end to end, for your size quilt.

	Sections
Wallhanging	4 sets of 2 sections
Crib	4 sets of 3 sections
Lap	2 sets of 4 sections and 2 sets of 3 sections

6. Lay out pieced strips with four sides of quilt. Starting with the sides, remove squares to match approximate length.

If the Pieced Border is too short: Trim all four sides of the First Border to that measurement.

If the Pieced Border is too long: Take a slightly deeper seam in several Pieced Border seams until it fits.

7. Pin and sew Pieced Borders to the sides.

8. Pin and sew Pieced Borders to top and bottom.

9. Turn to Finishing Your Quilt on page 104.

Fan Border for Quilts and Fan Table Runners

The Fan Borders and Table Runners follow the same techniques for assembling Fans. Punch out both sizes of Fan templates in back of book. For clarification, the Fans are referred to as Large Fans and Small Fans throughout this chapter.

Fan Border for Quilts: Refer to Fan Border in your yardage chart on page 25. Cut out all pieces as listed. Begin sewing on page 30.

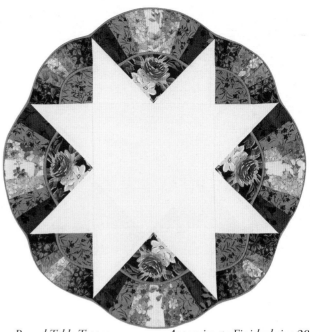

Round Table Topper   *Approximate Finished size 20"*

Round Table Topper Yardage

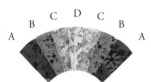

Fan Color 1 — Four Large Fans

A B C	⅛ yd each	
	(2) 4½" x 8" strips each	
D	⅛ yd	
	(1) 4½" x 8" strip	

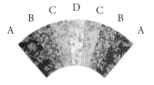

Fan Color 2 — Four Small Fans

A B C	⅛ yd each	
	(2) 4½" x 8" strips each	
D	⅛ yd	
	(1) 4½" x 8" strip	

Quarter Circles

Large Fans	¼ yd	or	4 Fussy Cut Flowers
Small Fans	⅛ yd		3" x 12"

Background

	1 yd	
	Backing	24" x 24"
	Corner Triangles	(4) 6" squares
	Center Square	Cut later, approximately 9" sq.

Piping, or Medium Rick Rack   (2) 2½ yd packages or 5 yds

Batting   Warm and Natural or Thermolam   24" x 24"

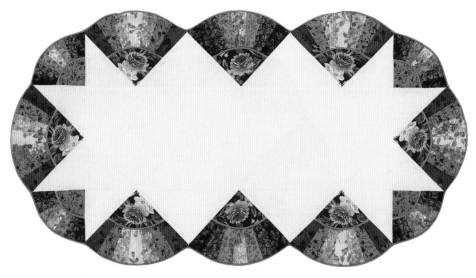

12 Fan Table Runner   *Approximate Finished size 20" x 36"*

12 Fan Table Runner Yardage ──────────────

Fan Color 1 — Six Large Fans

A B C	⅛ yd each
	(2) 4½" x 12" strips each
D	⅛ yd
	(1) 4½" x 12" strip

Fan Color 2 — Two Large Fans, Four Small Fans

A B C	⅛ yd each
	(2) 4½" x 12" strips each
D	⅛ yd
	(1) 4½" x 12" strip

Quarter Circles

| Large Fans | ¼ yd   or   8 Fussy Cut Flowers |
| Small Fans | ⅛ yd   3" x 12" |

Background   1⅜ yd

Backing	24" x 41"
Side Triangles	(1) 10" square
Corner Triangles	(4) 6" squares
Center Strip	Cut later, parallel to selvage
	approximately 9" x 26"

Piping or Medium Rick Rack   (2) 2½ yd packages or 5 yds

Batting   Warm and Natural or Thermolam   24" x 40"

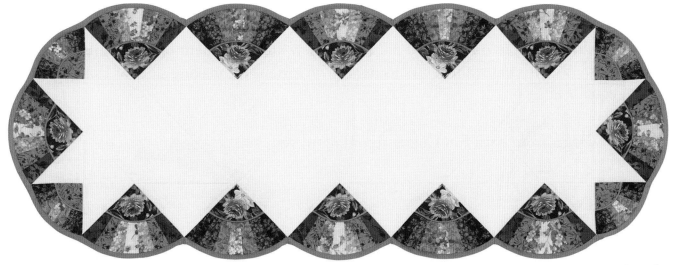

16 Fan Table Runner   *Approximate Finished Size 20" x 52"*

16 Fan Table Runner Yardage _____

Fan Color 1 — Eight Large Fans

A B C   ⅛ yd each
               (2) 4½" x 15" strips each

D   ⅛ yd
               (1) 4½" x 15" strip

Fan Color 2 — Four Large Fans, Four Small Fans

A B C   ⅛ yd each
               (2) 4½" x 15" strips each

D   ⅛ yd
               (1) 4½" x 15" strip

Quarter Circles

Large Fans   ¼ yd   or 12 Fussy Cut Flowers
Small Fans   ⅛ yd   3" x 12"

Background   2 yds

Backing   24" x 60"
Side Triangles   (2) 10" Squares
Corner Triangles   (4) 6" Squares
Center Strip   Cut later, parallel to selvage
                   approximately 9" x 43"

Piping, or Medium Rick Rack   (3) 2½ yd packages or 7½ yds

Batting   Warm and Natural or Thermolam   24" x 58"

Sewing Fans

1. Follow Fan directions on pages 30-37. **Do not sew embellishment onto assembled Wedges.** A consistent seam allowance is very important for making sides of Fans come out equal.

2. Trace Wedges from both Fan Colors according to your size.

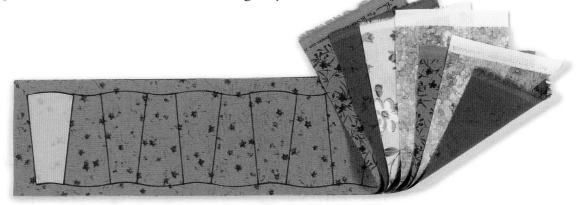

	Fan Color 1	Fan Color 2
Round Table Topper	4 Large Fans	4 Small Fans
12 Fan Table Runner	6 Large Fans	2 Large, 4 Small Fans
16 Fan Table Runner	8 Large Fans	4 Large, 4 Small Fans
Twin	16 Large Fans	13 Large, 4 Small Fans
Double/Queen	17 Large, 2 Small Fans	17 Large, 2 Small Fans
King	18 Large, 2 Small Fans	18 Large, 2 Small Fans

3. Sew embellishment of rick rack, piping, or lace on Quarter Circles only. **Do not sew embellishment onto assembled Wedges.**

4. **Do not sew Fans** onto Background Squares.

No embellishment

Embellishment

Positioning Quarter Circles

1. With a ruler, check a corner of your pressing mat or cutting mat for accuracy. *The center of your mat may be more accurate.*

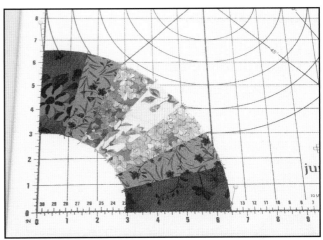

2. Place a Fan on that corner of your mat. Line up the two upper corners on the same measurements.

Depending on your seam allowance, the corners will fall approximately on the 6½ " measurement on large Fans and 4½ " on small Fans.

3. Position the Quarter Circle in the corner, overlapping the bottom edge of the Fan. Line up the straight sides with the lines on the mat.

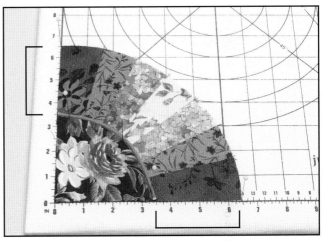

4. Place several fine pins standing straight up in the ditch on the embellishment.

Position Quarter Circle in corner and pin. Side measurements should be identical.

5. Pin the two outside edges, and then the center.

6. Stitch in the ditch around Quarter Circle embellishment with matching thread and needle down position. **Lengthen stitch** to 10 stitches per inch or 3.0.

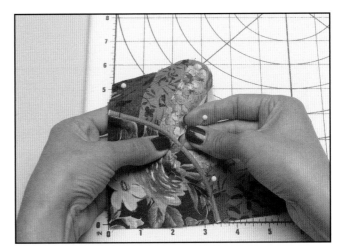

7. Assembly line sew all Quarter Circles to Fans.

Carefully lift up Fan and pin to Quarter Circle.

8. Sliver trim edges on any larger Fans.

Background Triangles

1. Cut 6" Background squares on one diagonal, making two Corner Triangles per square.

2. Stack and mark as Corner Triangles.

 Round Table Topper: Continue on page 86.

3. Cut 10" Background squares on both diagonals, making four Side Triangles per square.

4. Stack and mark as Side Triangles.

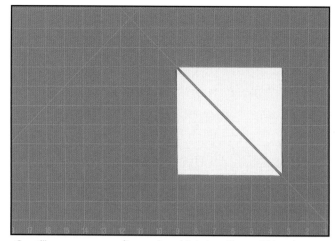

Cut 6" square on one diagonal and label as Corner Triangles.

Cut 10" square on on both diagonals, and label as Side Triangles.

	Corner Triangles	Side Triangles
Round Table Topper	(4) 6" squares	
12 Fan Table Runner	(4) 6" squares	(1) 10" square
16 Fan Table Runner	(4) 6" squares	(2) 10" squares
Twin	(3) 6" squares	(7) 10" squares
Double/Queen	(3) 6" squares	(8) 10" squares
King	(3) 6" squares	(9) 10" squares

Making Side Rows – Fan Border and Table Runners

1. Count out Fans for Sides.

	Color 1 Large	Small	Color 2 Large	Small
12 Fan Table Runner	4		2	4
16 Fan Table Runner	6		4	4
Twin	12		10	4
Double/Queen	12	2	12	2
King	12	2	12	2

2. Lay out two Sides with Large Fans. Begin and end sides with Corner Triangles and Side Triangles in between. Starting with Color 1, arrange Fans in alternating colors.

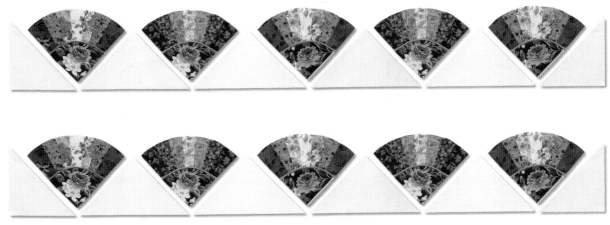

This is an example of a 16 Fan Table Runner.

3. Place this number of Fans for each Side.

	Fans
12 Fan Table Runner	3
16 Fan Table Runner	5
Twin	11
Double/Queen	12
King	12

Making Bottom Row – Fan Border for Quilts Only

1. Lay out Bottom row with remaining Large Fans in alternating colors. Begin and end with Corner Triangle.

2. Begin Twin row with Fan Color 1.

3. Begin Double/Queen and King rows with Fan Color 2.

4. Place this number of Fans in Bottom Row.

	Fans
Twin	7
Double/Queen	10
King	12

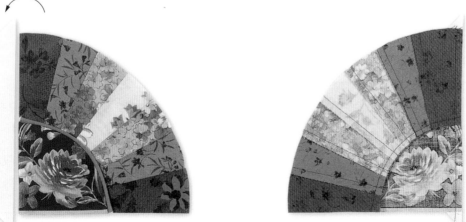

Example of Twin.

Sewing Rows Together – Fan Border and Table Runners

1. Begin on left end. Flip Fan right sides together to Corner Triangle and center. Triangle tips extend equally.

2. Sew to end of Fan. Repeat with second Side, and Bottom Row for quilts.

Sew to end of Fan.

3. **Rick rack or lace:** Steam press seams to Fan.

   Piping: Clip seam allowance just above the Quarter Circle. Steam press seams in opposite directions.

Clip piping just above seam allowance, and press seams in opposite directions.

4. Trim tip on bottom edge straight with side of Fan.

5. Flip a Side Triangle onto the Fan, lining up the square corner of the triangle with the upper right corner of the Fan.

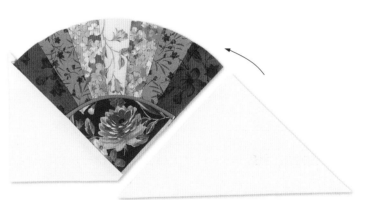

Trim tip straight with side of Fan before adding Side Triangle.

6. To avoid stretching bias edge, turn with Fan on top and bias edge on the bottom.

7. Sew end to end.

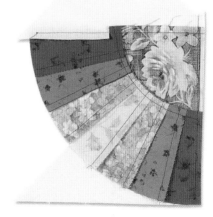

8. **Lace or Rick Rack:** Finger press seams to Fan.

Piping: Clip piping at Quarter Circle and press seam in opposite directions.

Clip piping and press seam in opposite directions.

9. Flip next Fan onto Side Triangle. Overlap top edge of the Fan by ¼". It should line up with the seam underneath.

10. Sew to end of Fan.

11. Continue with alternating Fan colors and Side Triangles. Sew all Fans. Trim tips straight with side of Fan.

12. Sew Corner Triangle to ends.

13. Steam press all seams.

14. Line up edge of ruler with the outside edge of Fan. Line up the ¼" ruler line with the bottom tip of Fan. Trim.

Table Runners Only: To calculate the length of Center Strip, measure the length of the assembled Fans.

Overlap top edge of the Fan by ¼".

Allow ¼" for seam allowance on bottom of Fan.

Length _____"

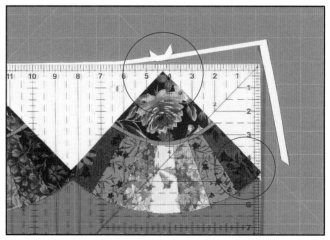

Line up right edge of ruler even with Fan.

Adding Small Fans on Corners of Sides

1. Flip a Small Fan in alternating color onto the right Corner Triangle.
   Line up top of Small Fan with top of Large Fan.

2. Sew to end of Fan.

This is an example of a 12 Fan Table Runner.

3. Sew Small Fan in alternating color on opposite side. Steam press seams towards
   Fans, or clip above piping and press in opposite directions.

This is an example of a 16 Fan Table Runner.

Fan Quilt: Continue on page 91.

Making Ends – Round Table Topper and Table Runners

1. Center and flip Fan Color 1 onto Corner Triangle with tips extending.

Center Fan on Corner Triangle.

2. Sew to end of Fan.

3. **Lace or Rick Rack:** Finger press seams to Fan.

   Piping: Clip piping at Quarter Circle and press seam in opposite directions. See first photo on page 83.

Round Table Topper: Make four identical Ends.

Table Runners: Make a second identical End.

4. Trim tip on bottom edge straight with side of Fan.

5. Center and sew a second Corner Triangle to the opposite side.

6. Press seam toward Fan, or clip piping and press in opposite directions.

Trim tip on bottom edge straight with side of Fan.

7. Turn Fan upside down. With a 12½" Square Up ruler, line up right edge of ruler with right edge of Fan.

8. Line up bottom tip of the Fan at ¼" line on ruler. Trim two sides.

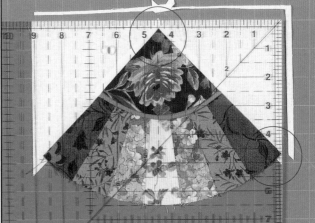

Line up right edge of ruler even with Fan.

9. Turn Fan right side up. Line up remaining side of Fan with ruler and trim right edge.

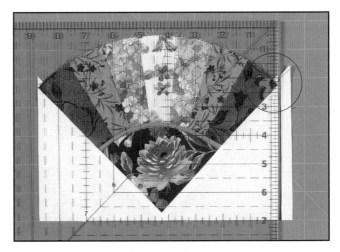

Line up right edge of ruler even with Fan.

10. To calculate the width of Center Square for Table Topper or Center Strip for Table Runners, measure the width of this piece. It should measure approximately 8½" to 8¾" across.

Width _____"

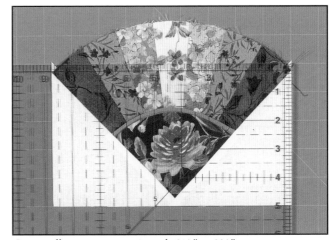

Piece will measure approximately 8½" to 8¾" across.

Sewing Table Topper Together

1. Flip a Small Fan onto each side of Corner Triangles. Line up top of Small Fan with top of Large Fan. Line up bottom edges.

2. Sew end to end on Fan.

3. Make two identical Side Pieces.

Make two identical Side Pieces.

4. Press seams toward Fan, or clip piping and press in opposite directions.

5. Cut a Center Square the size of your End recorded on page 87.

6. Sew Center Square to two remaining Ends. Press seams to Center Square.

7. Pin Sides in place, matching seams at Corner Fans. Stitch, and press seams to Center Square.

8. Sew embellishment to outside edge, overlapping ends.

9. Turn to **Finishing Table Runners** on page 90.

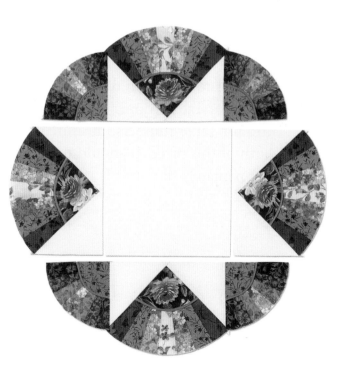

Sewing Table Runner Together

1. To calculate the size of your Center Strip, take recorded length on page 84 and recorded width on page 87.

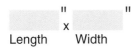
Length   x   Width

2. Cut strip according to your measurements.

3. Lay out Center Strip with Sides and End Pieces.

4. Sew Ends on first, and press seams toward Center Strip.

5. Pin Sides in place, matching up seams at Corner Fans.

6. Sew, and press seams towards Center Strip.

7. **Sew embellishment around outside edge,** overlapping ends.

Optional: Finish outside edge with extra wide double fold bias tape after Table Runner is quilted.

16 Fan Table Runner Example

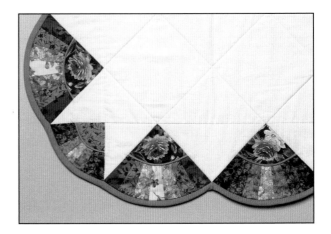

Finishing Table Runners

1. Pin Table Runner and Backing right sides together. Following the embellishment stitches, sew outside edge. Leave one large Fan unstitched for turning. Trim outside edge of Backing. Clip inside points.

2. Cut batting to same size as Table Runner. Hand baste batting to outside edge of Table Runner. Turn right side out through opening. Hand stitch opening closed.

3. Line up a 6" x 24" ruler diagonally with opposite Fans. With a Hera Marker, mark creases for machine quilting.

4. Pin layers together with 1" safety pins.

5. Place walking foot on machine. Set stitch length at 10 stitches per inch or 3.0.

6. With matching thread, stitch in the ditch continuously on creased lines.

7. Stitch in the ditch around Center Strip.

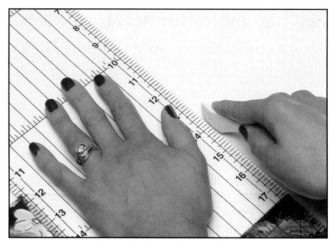

Mark diagonal creases with hera marker.

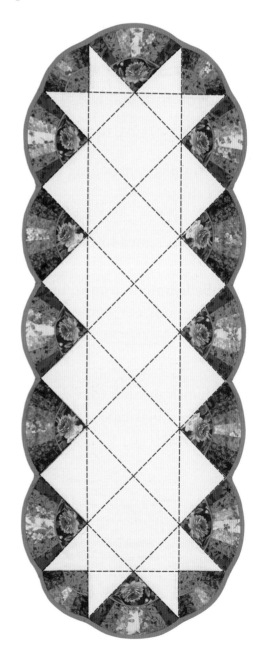

Fan Border for Quilts

Calculating Width of Wide Border Strips

1. Lay out Bottom Row of Fans next to bottom
   edge of quilt top and measure lengths of both.

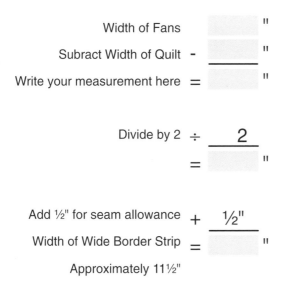

Width of Fans		"
Subract Width of Quilt	−	"
Write your measurement here	=	"
Divide by 2	÷	2
	=	"
Add ½" for seam allowance	+	½"
Width of Wide Border Strip	=	"
Approximately 11½"		

2. Cut this many Wide Border Strips,
   selvage to selvage, for your size quilt.

	Wide Strips
Twin	6
Double/Queen	7
King	7

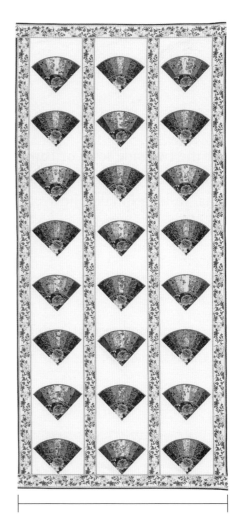

3. Sew Wide Border on two sides and bottom edge only. Refer to **Adding First Border** on page 55.

4. Pin and sew bottom row of Fans along bottom edge of quilt top. Press seams towards quilt.

Calculating Width of Top Border Strip

1. Measure the length of the quilt from the top edge to the Bottom Edge of Corner Triangle.

2. Lay out the two side rows of Fans next to one another. Measure the length from end to end. If the two sides are not equal in length, take the average length.

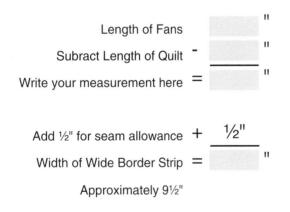

Length of Fans		"
Subract Length of Quilt	-	"
Write your measurement here	=	"
Add ½" for seam allowance	+	½"
Width of Wide Border Strip	=	"
Approximately 9½"		

3. Cut this many Top Wide Border Strips,
   selvage to selvage, for your size quilt.

	Wide Strips
Twin	2
Double/Queen	3
King	3

4. Square ends and sew strips together.

5. Sew the Wide Border Strips to top edge.

6. Pin side rows of Fans in place, matching
   seams at Corner Fan. Stitch and press seams
   toward quilt.

7. Layer and quilt following directions on
   pages 104 - 106. **Do not trim Batting
   and Backing.**

8. Turn to page 94 for
   Making Facing for Quilt with Fan Border.

Making Facing for Quilt with Fan Border

1. Thread machine with color of bobbin thread that contrasts with Backing. With 10 stitches per inch, or 3.0, machine baste Fan Border ¼" from outside edge. Stop and pivot at corner of Fans.

2. Sew 7" facing strips together and cut to lengths of top, bottom, and two sides of quilt.

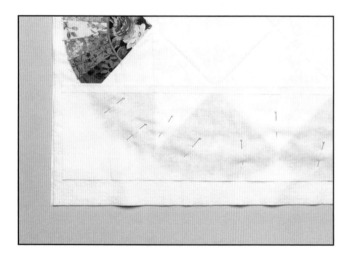

3. Press under ¼" and stitch one long edge of each facing strip.

4. With right sides together, line up the raw edge of facing strips with two sides of quilt. Place pins in from outside edge of Fans.

5. Place facing strips on top and bottom edges, overlapping side strips in corners.

6. Turn quilt with Backing on top, and stitch along outside edge just inside basting stitches.

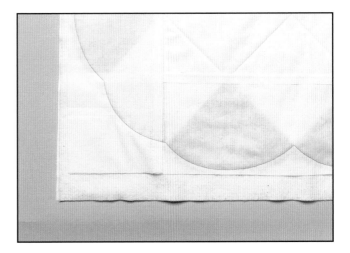

7. Trim Batting, Backing, and Facing from outside edge. Clip at inside curves.

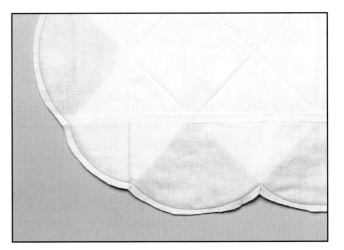

8. Turn facing to back of Quilt and finger-press outside edges.

9. Pin inside curves first, perpendicular to edge. Pin along Fan.

10. Blind hem stitch edge of facing to Backing.

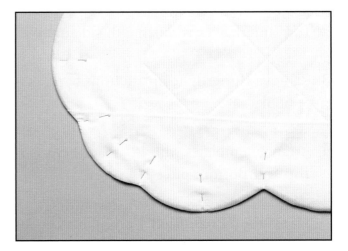

Making Butterfly Appliques

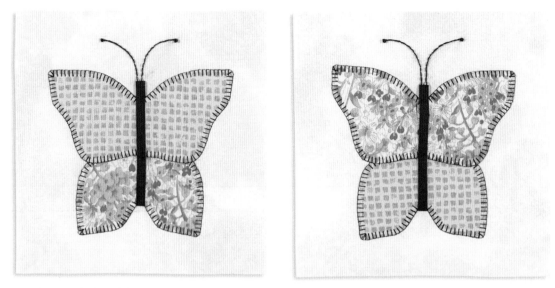

Make two butterflies at a time. The examples were machine sewn. If preferred, outside edges may be hand blind stitched or hand blanket stitched after bias tape is inserted.

1. Count out this many pairs of coordinating 6½" fabric squares and fusible interfacing.

	Fabric	Interfacing
Wallhanging	6 total or 3 pairs	6
Crib	16 total or 8 pairs	16
Lap	18 total or 9 pairs	18
Twin	24 total or 12 pairs	24
Double/Queen	40 total or 20 pairs	40
King	48 total or 24 pairs	48

2. Turn interfacing with smooth side up.

3. Remove Butterfly template from back of book.

4. Arrange templates with ½" space between Top and Bottom pieces.

5. Trace around templates with fine point permanent pen.

6. Place rough, fusible side of interfacing against right side of two squares of coordinating fabrics. Pin.

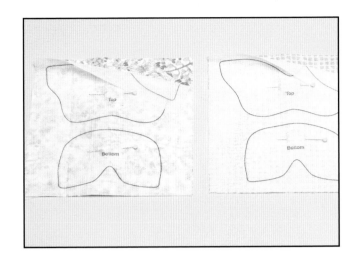

7. With 20 stitches per inch or 1.5 on computerized machines, sew on drawn lines.

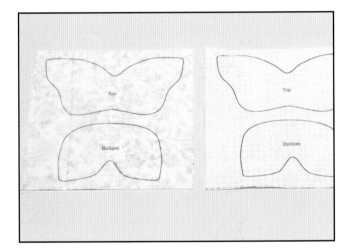

8. Cut Top and Bottom pieces apart. Trim seams to ⅛". Clip inside curves.

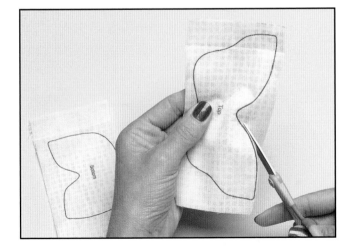

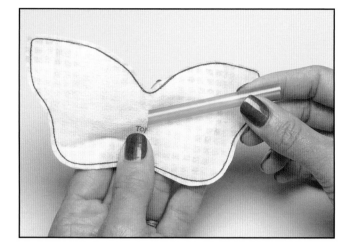

9. Cut a small opening in center of interfacing on each piece.

10. Cut fat drinking straw in half. Insert straw into hole. Push straw against fabric.

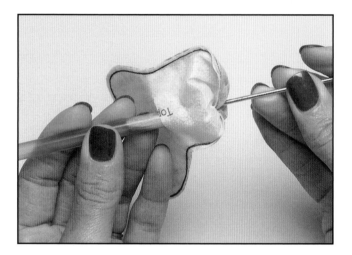

11. Place ball of bodkin on fabric stretched over straw, and gently push fabric into straw with bodkin. This begins to turn the piece.

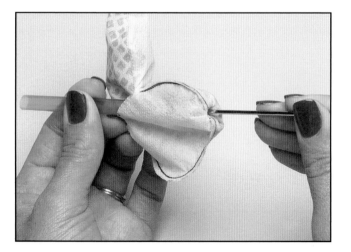

12. Remove straw and bodkin. Insert straw in second half, and turn right side out.

13. Run round end of bodkin around inside edge, pushing out seams.

14. From right side use a pin or stiletto to pull out points.

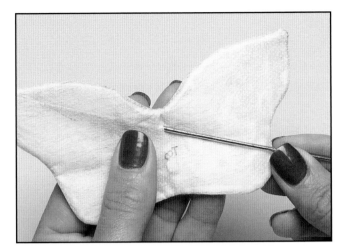

15. From right side, push fabric over interfacing edge with wooden iron.

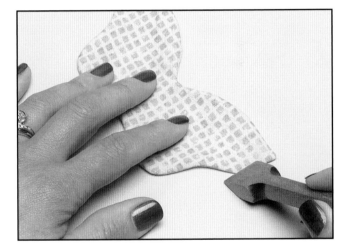

16. Cut cotton batting same size as butterfly pieces. Insert batting through opening with hemostats.

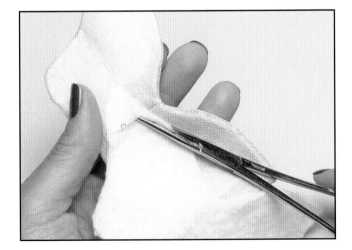

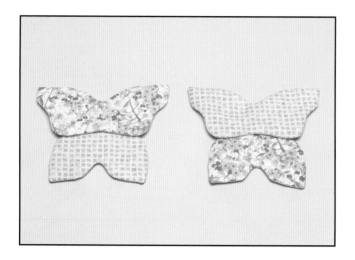

17. Switch Tops to make two different Butterflies.

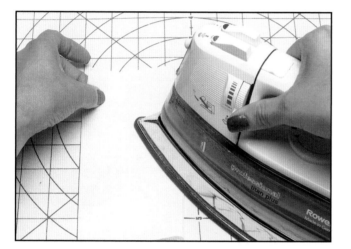

18. Fold 7" Background Square in half and press center crease.

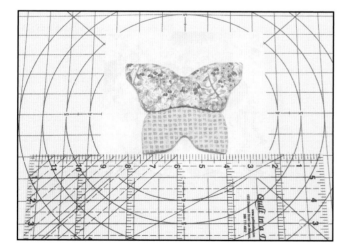

19. Measure 1" up from bottom edge and position center of Bottom piece on center crease.

20. Center and position Top piece overlapping Bottom piece by ¼".

21. From right side, steam press one half of the Butterfly at a time. Leave the center unpressed to allow for bias tape. Turn to wrong side and press sides again.

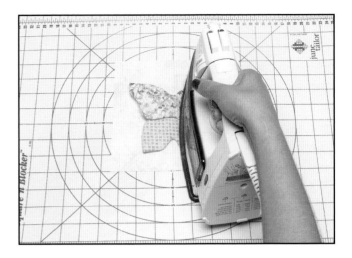

22. Choose black thread for machine blanket stitch, or invisible thread for blind hem stitch. Peel back lower edges of Top piece to conceal beginning and ending stitches. Stitch along the outside edge of the Bottom piece, leaving ⅜" unstitched at the center.

Leave center open.

23. Cut fusible bias tape into 6" lengths. With the flat end of a bodkin or a stiletto, slip one end of the tape under the top center opening. The fusible side should be up. Begin machine stitching on the tape, and continue sewing the outside edge.

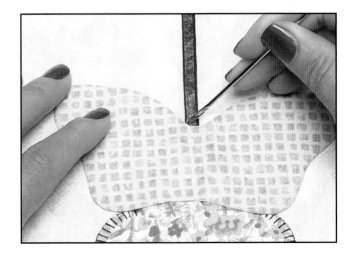

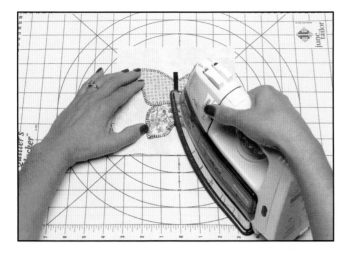

24. With the bodkin or stiletto, slip the other end of the tape into the opening at the bottom.

25. Press bias tape in place, allowing a small "head" to extend on top. Hand or machine stitch edges of bias tape.

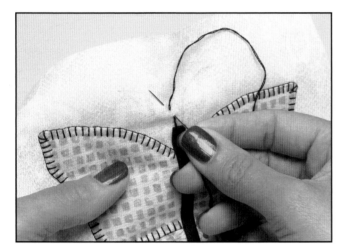

26. With a pencil, draw two arcs above the head for antennas. With two strands of embroidery floss, backstitch along the drawn lines. Make French knots on the ends of the antennas.

27. Optional embellishments include sewing buttons or yo-yos onto the wings.

28. Turn to page 43 for **Sewing Blocks Together.**

Patterns

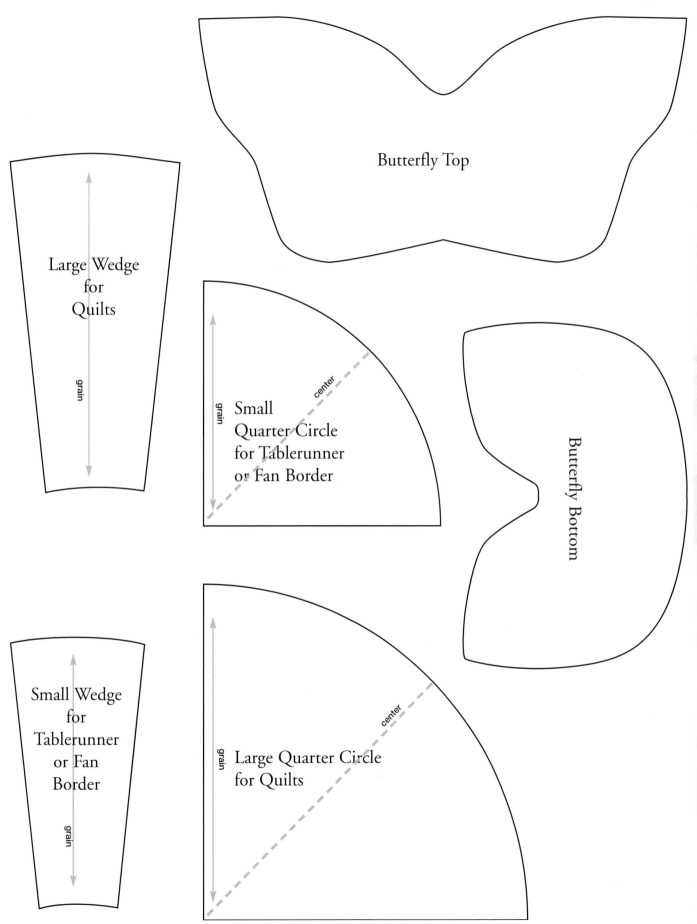

Large Wedge
for
Quilts

grain

Butterfly Top

Small
Quarter Circle
for Tablerunner
or Fan Border

grain

center

Butterfly Bottom

Small Wedge
for
Tablerunner
or Fan
Border

grain

Large Quarter Circle
for Quilts

grain

center

Finishing Your Quilt

Layering the Quilt

1. Spread out Backing on a large table or floor area, right side down. Clamp fabric to edge of table with quilt clips, or tape Backing to the floor. Do not stretch Backing.

2. Layer the Batting on the Backing and pat flat.

3. With quilt right side up, center on the Backing. Smooth until all layers are flat. Clamp or tape outside edges.

Safety Pinning

1. Place pin covers on 1" safety pins. Safety pin through all layers three to five inches apart. Pin away from where you plan to quilt.

2. Catch tip of pin in grooves on pinning tool, and close pins.

3. Use pinning tool to open pins when removing them. Store pins opened.

"Stitch in the Ditch" along Lattice, Triangles and Borders

1. Thread your machine with matching thread or invisible thread. If you use invisible thread, loosen your top tension. Match the bobbin thread to the Backing.

2. Attach your walking foot, and lengthen the stitch to 8 to 10 stitches per inch or 3.5 on computerized machines.

3. Tightly roll quilt from one long side to center vertical Lattice. Place hands on quilt in triangular shape, and spread seams open. Stitch in the ditch along seam lines.

4. Continue working from the center to outside Lattice, unrolling one row at a time. Sew all rows in same direction.

5. Roll opposite side and sew remaining Lattice in one direction. Sew top and bottom Lattice.

6. Working in a zig-zag direction, stitch along Triangles, pivoting and turning with needle down.

7. Continue quilting until all Borders are stitched. For added dimension, stitch ¼" inside edge of Triangles.

8. Using walking foot as a guide, stitch ¼" from top edge of Fan. Stitch in the ditch along top edge of Quarter Circle.

Amie Potter enhanced the beauty of this quilt with free motion medallions in the lattice, channel quilting on the scallop borders, and background stippling for interest.

Award winning quilter, Carol Selepec free-motion quilted graceful feathers in the Wide Border, and quilted ¼" from Fans.

Quilting with Darning Foot

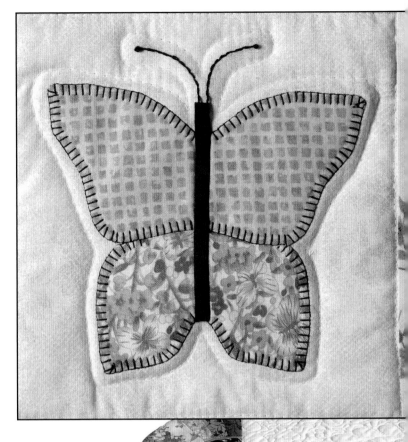

1. To echo quilt the Butterfly, attach darning foot to sewing machine. Drop feed dogs or cover feed dogs with a plate. No stitch length is required as you control the length. Use a fine needle and invisible or regular thread in the top and regular thread to match the Backing in the bobbin. Loosen top tension if using invisible thread.

2. Place hands flat on sides of Butterfly. Bring bobbin thread up ¼" from outside edge of Butterfly. Lock stitch and clip thread tails. Free motion stitch ¼" around Butterfly. Lock stitch and cut threads. Continue with remaining blocks.

For extra dimension Carol Selepec free motion quilted feathers in the Wide Border and filled in the background with stippling.

Binding

Use a walking foot attachment and regular thread on top and in the bobbin to match the Binding.

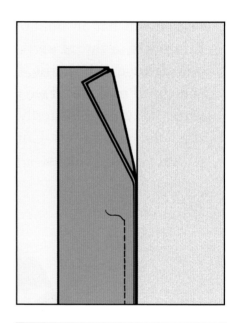

1. Square off the selvage edges, and sew 2¾" Binding strips together lengthwise.

2. Fold and press in half with wrong sides together.

3. Line up the raw edges of the folded Binding with the raw edges of the quilt in the middle of one side.

4. Begin stitching 4" from the end of the Binding. Sew with 10 stitches per inch, or 3.0 to 3.5. Sew ⅜" from edge, or width of walking foot.

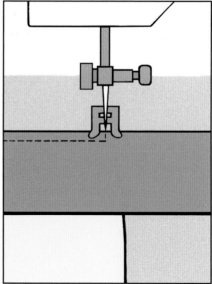

5. At the corner, stop the stitching ⅜" in from the edge with the needle in the fabric. Raise the presser foot and turn the quilt to the next side. Put the foot back down.

6. Stitch backwards off the edge of the Binding.

7. Stitch backwards off the edge of the Binding, raise the foot, and pull the quilt forward slightly.

8. Fold the Binding strip straight up on the diagonal. Fingerpress the diagonal fold.

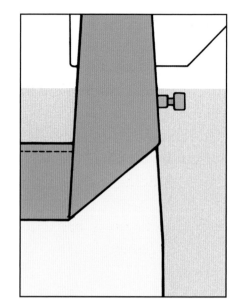

9. Fold the Binding strip straight down with the diagonal fold underneath. Line up the top of the fold with the raw edge of the Binding underneath.

10. Begin sewing from the edge.

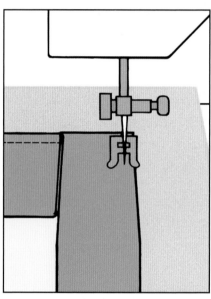

11. Continue stitching and mitering the corners around the outside of the quilt.

12. Stop stitching 4" from where the ends will overlap.

13. Line up the two ends of Binding. Trim the excess with a ½" overlap.

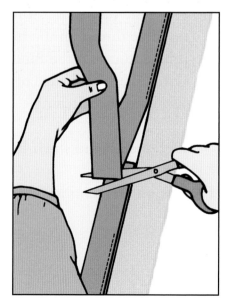

14. Open out the folded ends and pin right sides together. Sew a ¼" seam.

15. Continue to stitch the Binding in place.

16. Trim the Batting and Backing up to the raw edges of the Binding.

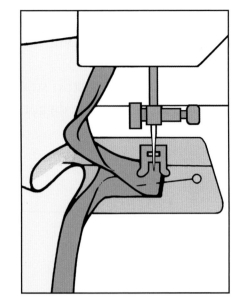

17. Fold the Binding to the back side of the quilt. Pin in place so that the folded edge on the Binding lines up with the stitching line. Tuck in the excess fabric at each miter on the diagonal.

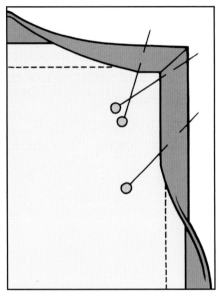

18. From the right side, "stitch in the ditch" using invisible thread on the front side, and bobbin thread to match the Binding on the back side. Catch the folded edge of the Binding on the back side with the stitching.

Optional: Hand stitch Binding in place.

19. Sew on an identification label on the Back.

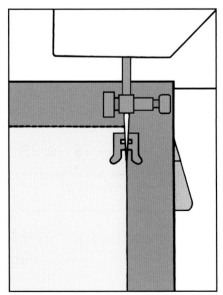

Index

Quilt in a Day®, Inc.
1955 Diamond Street, San Marcos, California 92069
phone 800 777-4852 • fax 760 591-4424
www.quiltinaday.com

This Page

Cotton prints by Benartex provide a wealth of creative possibilities for your quilts. On this day bed quilt, fan blocks in purple and blue prints are framed by medium scale floral strips and a small scale floral background from the same line. The large scale floral of the outer border also supplied the "fussy cut" roses for the fan blocks. Quilt by Patricia Knoechel, machine quilted by Carol Selepec.

Facing Page

Appliquéd butterflies and spring-time flowers are a cheerful addition to Melissa Varnes' room. Using a fabric line such as Rainbow Florals by Benartex makes it easy to create coordinated quilts and wallhangings for home decorating. Quilt and wallhanging by Patricia Knoechel, machine quilted by Carol Selepec.

Back Cover

By selecting dark, rich hues of blues and reds on a tone on tone background, Patricia Knoechel created her beautiful Asian fan quilt. She embellished the fans and scallop border with black rickrack to create a striking effect, and finished the borders with an oriental influenced print fabric. Quilted by Amie Potter.